GRATITUDE
Tiger

Also by Joel Zuckerman

Golf in the Lowcountry—2003

Golf Charms of Charleston—2005

Misfits on the Links—2006

A Hacker's Humiliations—2007

Pete Dye Golf Courses: Fifty Years of Visionary Design—2008**

Pro's Pros—2011**

Kiawah Golf: The Game's Elegant Island—2013

Golfers Giving Back—2015

Grateful—2020

**Denotes Book of the Year as bestowed by
the International Network of Golf

GRATITUDE
Tiger

JOEL ZUCKERMAN

Creating Joy Through
the Art of Impactful Letters

FOREWORD BY
OLYMPIC SKI LEGEND PICABO STREET

GREENLEAF
BOOK GROUP PRESS

Published by Greenleaf Book Group Press
Austin, Texas
www.gbgpress.com

Distributed by Greenleaf Book Group

For ordering information or special discounts for bulk purchases,
please contact Greenleaf Book Group at PO Box 91869, Austin, TX
78709, 512.891.6100.

Design and composition by Greenleaf Book Group
Cover design by Michelle Rayner

Publisher's Cataloging-in-Publication data is available.

Print ISBN: 979-8-88645-332-4

eBook ISBN: 979-8-88645-333-1

To offset the number of trees consumed in the printing of our books,
Greenleaf donates a portion of the proceeds from each printing to
the Arbor Day Foundation. Greenleaf Book Group has replaced over
50,000 trees since 2007.

Printed in the United States of America on acid-free paper

25 26 27 28 29 30 31 32   10 9 8 7 6 5 4 3 2 1

First Edition

Dedicated to Leslie, Jack, and Ethan,
to whom I am deeply (fiercely?) grateful.

Contents

Foreword

by Picabo Street

My life until now has taken a hundred-and-something twists and turns, many of which were completely unexpected. Writing the foreword to this book is just another twist!

I'm going to write about gratitude, tigers, and lastly, the Gratitude Tiger.

Where do I even begin regarding gratitude?

I'm grateful and appreciative that I was raised by unusual parents in a unique environment. My dad was a Marine-turned-hippie, a chef-turned-stonemason, and my mom was a musician, accountant, and writer. They insisted that chores had to be completed before playtime, and the work ethic they instilled from an early age carried me forward to the athletic success that came later.

I'm glad I was the *only girl in my town*, just a wide spot in the road called Triumph, Idaho (population: 33). Every day I tried to keep up with my older brother and the other boys in the neighborhood. There were no dolls or dress-up. It was rough-and-tumble, with BB guns, bikes, football, Friday night fights, and war games. It helped develop and hone my competitive edge.

I'm grateful for the people who believed in me, such as my coaches and mentors. I'm grateful for the fact that my skiing ability was discovered early and was nurtured, which ultimately allowed me to travel the world from a town with fewer residents than are currently living on your block. I'm grateful for the expert medical care I received and the full recoveries I was able to make after devastating injuries. I'm grateful I made an enduring mark on the sport of skiing.

I'm grateful I have three wonderful sons. I'm grateful the Picabo Street Academy in Park City, Utah, services young athletes in need of flexible academic schedules. It makes me happy they don't have to endure what I did—traveling the world with an overstuffed backpack full of textbooks, trying to keep up with high school studies while training and competing against the best skiers in the world.

I'm sometimes grateful, sometimes less so, regarding my unusual name. One thing that's hard to argue—it's certainly memorable! In short, I'm grateful for this whole roller-coaster ride I've experienced.

Regarding tigers: At the 1993 World Cup in Japan, I was coveting a sweatshirt owned by Swiss/Luxembourg skier Marc Girardelli. He told me, "Make it onto the podium tomorrow, and it's yours." (By the way, Girardelli was no stranger to ski racing success. He made it onto the podium *one hundred times* and won a pair of Olympic medals during his long career.) Anyway, I made the podium, and when he gave me the sweatshirt, he referred to me as a tiger.

Subsequently, five years later, in 1998, my helmet artist John Blackman painted me a tiger, unprompted, because on the Chinese calendar, it was the Year of the Tiger. He had previously produced helmets for me with an Idaho landscape, Medusa, a globe, a ram's horns, and so on. With my tiger helmet strapped on firmly, I was fortunate enough to win Olympic gold in the Super G in Nagano, Japan.

As you'll learn in the book chapter "Gratitude TIGER," the author has his own gratitude-centric acronym for the word TIGER. But this is my personal interpretation:

T is for Tenacity.
I is for Integrity.
G is for Gratitude.
E is for Expectation.
R is for Respect.

I have attempted to live by all five tenets, so as you can imagine, I've always been partial to tigers!

Joel Zuckerman is a tiger in his own right, and I'm also partial to him. Imagine—writing nearly three hundred Letters of Gratitude to individuals near and far! I laughed when he told me about a reoccurring comment he receives from amazed audience members after a speaking presentation: "Three hundred letters? I don't think I know three hundred people!"

The fact is, I've written plenty of letters myself. My dad insisted I write to sponsors and those who helped me when I was young. I even wrote a "Public Letter of Gratitude." It was published in the *Sun Valley Mountain Express* in the early '80s, after I returned with an armload of medals from the Junior Olympics in Alaska. I thanked all the businesses around town individually and by name that had donated to help me make my way to the event.

I never stop trying to improve myself, and I think letter writing is a form of self-care. You develop an intimate connection with and create a cherished keepsake for the person to whom you write. So, apparently Joel has been "intimate" with nearly three hundred people, couples, and groups, but hey—who am I to judge?

In my opinion, this one-on-one expression of gratitude allows your gratitude to flower and bloom and reach other parts of your life. Using your tiger tenets, you can find it in any place and in every place if you develop the right mindset.

This book is a mix of sage advice, examples of effective letter-writing techniques, funny incidents, unique perspectives, poignant moments, unexpected repercussions, and a wide range of concepts to help you improve your ability to show gratitude to others. And by showing this love and appreciation to *others*, you are simultaneously showing love and appreciation to *yourself*.

I'm not a golfer. Therefore, I've never been exposed to Joel's many books on the subject, popular as they are. But I'm "grateful" he has now chosen to focus on showing us how to effectively express our gratitude. Which, in my opinion, is far more important than golf, and, for that matter, skiing!

Read onward and learn how you can become a Gratitude Tiger yourself.

Introduction

The purpose of this slender volume is to illustrate that taking up the hobby of writing Letters of Gratitude to those who've been important, instrumental, and continuously (or previously) in one's corner is a life-changing, and life-affirming experience.

My expertise in this subject has nothing to do with an advanced educational degree, as there is none in my possession. Nor can a deep understanding of psychology be claimed, because that is also nonexistent.

There is a single element on my resume that affords a certain authority to discuss these matters with enlightenment. I have written nearly three hundred Letters of Gratitude in the last decade. It has changed and bettered me in countless ways. By extending myself to others, it results in me being better to myself, and a better person in general.

The pages that follow showcase a wide range of benefits and results from taking up this enriching, endearing hobby. They won't be belabored here because the table of contents is self-explanatory. Suffice it to say that *Gratitude Tiger* is meant to serve a dual purpose.

In some ways it's a "how-to" on getting started writing letters to those in your orbit. As importantly, it's also a "why" book. There are numerous reasons to consider reaching out in this delightful, heartfelt, and permanent manner. The pages that follow will outline and hone in on these myriad benefits.

This rare amalgamation of eccentricity, effusiveness, monomania, and vast life circle, from both the present and past, have resulted in the sizeable sheaf of letters in my personal archive. Stacked up, they would resemble more than half a ream of paper one would purchase at an office supply store.

There are no illusions harbored that any reader, no matter their level of enthusiasm, will write several hundred Letters of Gratitude. But perhaps there'll be a smattering of self-starters who will write dozens of letters, or at least a handful. No matter the number, there is no doubt that a sense of joy and accomplishment will accompany each and every communication written and sent; the final tally isn't relevant.

Enjoy this unusual book! I'm "grateful" you'll consider making this hobby your own.

1

The Metamorphosis

(with Apologies to Franz Kafka)

There was once a time, and for quite a long time, I was a busy, often up-to-my-elbows golf-and-travel writer. I was also something of an ingrate, but more on that in a bit.

In the fall of 1997, circumstances allowed me to fall ass-backward into a work gig that changed my career fortunes drastically. Despite not having written much more than a grocery list in fifteen years, I landed (actually talked my way into) a job as the golf columnist for the *Carolina Morning News* on Hilton Head Island, South Carolina. Up until that point, there had been a half dozen different careers I had tried on and rejected like so many ill-fitting suits.

There's a classic line from *Wayne's World*—the great 1992 Mike Myers–Dana Carvey comedy—that has always resonated with me. Said a self-reflective Wayne, "I've had plenty of jobs, but nothing I'd call a career. Let me put it this way: I have an extensive collection of nametags and hairnets."[1]

I wasn't *quite* on that "fast food, working at the mall" level, but there had been a certain amount of flailing employment-wise, lasting more than a decade.

My columnist job in one of golf's great meccas garnered attention, and I quickly leveled up, finding steady magazine work. First local, then regional, then airline, then national. In addition, websites were proliferating, and more eyeballs were online every year. That additional exposure eventually led to book contracts. My first hardcover was published in 2003 and begat several others quickly—during the most prolific period, there were five brand-new titles on bookshelves within six years. My speaking career followed a similar trajectory: modest beginnings at Rotary Clubs and ladies' luncheons, and, within a few years as my profile rose, corporate events, conferences, country clubs, and luxury cruise lines.

Within a year of my debut newspaper column (January 1, 1998) and for the following twenty, I received numerous press junkets invitations issued annually—three- to five-day, even weeklong, jamborees where a resort, municipality, state, or even a country's tourism board would invite select writers to indulge in their hospitality. The hosts assumed that by putting on the ritz (occasionally at the Ritz) for the journalists, fawning coverage would ensue. They weren't wrong.

---

1   Wayne Campbell (played by Mike Myers), *Wayne's World*, Penelope Spheeris, director, Paramount Pictures, 1992.

The existential problem was that within a year or so of these boondoggles commencing, this "quasi-celebrity" lifestyle was taken completely for granted. There was a traveling circus of fifty to one hundred writers (sometimes interspersed with television and radio personalities) on this "golf gravy train," and I saw many of the same faces as I hopscotched about, both domestically and overseas. Some events involved just four or five writers, while others were fifteen or fifty. We descended on these locales, be they exotic or mundane, as if we were rock stars, though we didn't have the fame, talent, money, or groupies—just the sense of entitlement.

As I look back, there must've been numerous occasions when I thanked the lucky stars above for this crazy kaleidoscope of a life that had appeared out of thin air, but probably not that often. The first trip, a state-sponsored six- or seven-day self-drive with two other writers through the golf wilds of Minnesota, was like being a kid in a candy store. But after just two or three additional trips, maybe a year from that initial foray, it was de rigueur . . . just my job. I slipped into this "alternate universe" as easily as one would slip into a favorite pair of sandals.

I do remember being put off by crack-of-dawn flights, having to connect at an airline hub when they could've flown me direct, schlepping the "rolling coffin" (i.e., the golf travel bag on wheels) through what seemed like miles of disjointed airport terminals, unpleasant golf pairings with fellow scribes or tourism officials who were partially or wholly objectionable, patchy fairways lacking grass, uninspiring, run-of-the-mill golf facilities where mustering a complimentary paragraph or two would be an arduous task, city (or spa, or hotel) tours in which there wasn't a whit of interest, cocktail hours that seemed too short, extravagant dinners that went on too long, and so on. Talk about entitled!

In the autumn of 2013, while still actively engaged in these professional writing and speaking endeavors, I took notice of a book on my wife's nightstand. A huge bestseller in the 1990s, *Don't Sweat the Small Stuff* by the late Richard Carlson was a series of tips, tricks, and hacks to living a better, more enriching life. These were microchapters, two or three pages long, and one in particular that stood out was titled "Write a Heartfelt Letter." I decided to take on the challenge, purely as an intellectual exercise.

That very afternoon, I pecked out a letter on my computer to a colleague, mentor, and friend named Dan Shepherd. He had been instrumental in my writing life in many ways, including facilitating at least a dozen of these previously described boondoggles. After requesting his address, hunting for a stamp and envelope, sashaying to the mailbox, and flicking it through the slot, the experiment seemed complete. Truth be told, when sitting down to write that letter, it never occurred there would be a second one forthcoming.

However, I was taken aback by the feeling of warmth and accomplishment that coursed through me shortly after depositing the envelope into the mailbox. It was surprising, this depth of feeling that ensued by sharing positive thoughts and deep gratitude to someone important. So, a week later, another letter went into the mailbox. Then another and another. Within a year, the pile had grown to twenty. It's a fact that a year or more later, the milestone fiftieth also included a small handful of confetti in the envelope!

After some four years, the pile of letters had reached triple digits. A few years later, at 150 letters, I had an epiphany. I decided to compose an additional thirty letters, and, upon reaching 180 letters written and sent, compiled the entire collection into a book, which I titled *Grateful*. I approached this organically, with no rush, and it took another eighteen months to hit the magic number—to get from 150 all the way to 180.

My previous eight books were commercially available, some more successful and attention-getting than others. But *Grateful* was not for public consumption. It was distributed as a gift to many (not all) of those who had previously received letters. It was an homage to the many relationships, old and new, deeper and more casual, that had been developed and fostered over the decades.

The book was lovely, nearly four hundred pages in length, hardbound, and tastefully produced. It met all expectations, and (particularly as a professional critic for all those years) that's not a phrase tossed about with impunity. A small part of me thought this letter-writing phase had reached its conclusion.

However, it turned out that it was just a small part of me. Because a month after the book's debut, Ed Stambovsky, my long-time accountant, golf buddy, and family friend, passed away after a long illness. I had written to him previously, and the letter was featured in the book, but now there was a compulsion to write a Letter of Gratitude/Condolence to his widow.

Not two months later, an Instagram message came completely out of the blue. It was from a woman friend of mine, Karen Massimino, who had disappeared into the ether some thirty-five years earlier! We had a few delightful catch-up phone conversations in the weeks following. Soon she was in receipt of a Letter of Gratitude, thanking her for reappearing from thin air and for the youthful hijinks of decades past. Anyway, the writing continued, slowly at first, then with more momentum.

As of the writing of this chapter, more than eighty-five

additional letters have been created and mailed since *Grateful* was published late in 2020, bringing the total close to 300. In my mind, there's no scenario imaginable where losing interest in this remarkably uplifting hobby could occur. One might logically conclude that eventually the well will run dry, and there'll be no more people to write to. But it's become such an essential part of me, and as people continue to inspire, befriend, positively influence, or provide a kindness, they'll hear about it in this uniquely endearing manner. Parenthetically, I no longer speak professionally about golf—only on the many emotional and psychological benefits of expressive or proactive gratitude.

It's no coincidence that the energy directed toward this hobby-turned-vocation is directly correlated to the denouement of the golf-writing world. Pay scales started to plunge in the years following the 2008 financial meltdown, slowly at first, and then at an accelerated pace. Interesting writing opportunities diminished concurrently. But the hard truth is there had been a saturation point with golf. Everything I needed or wanted to say about the game had been said.

Put it this way: The nine books prior to this one total some two thousand pages. Add to that nearly one thousand features, travelogues, and profiles for more than one hundred magazines, websites, and newspapers, averaging slightly more than three pages in length. The total combination of all this professional work—the books and feature pieces combined—total five thousand pages. But the nearly three hundred Letters of Gratitude written to date, which is a little more than 5 percent of my professional output, are *far* more important than any thoughts I ever typed, be they original or regurgitated, about that ancient stick-and-ball game.

There's plenty of unique information, much of it entertaining, poignant, useful, and thought-provoking in the pages to come. But these opening remarks will conclude with ten simple words, just two basic sentences, the absolute essence of what's to come:

Write Letters of Gratitude. It will make *you* feel good.

2

Defining a Letter of Gratitude

Considering this entire volume is a discussion of the joys and benefits of writing Letters of Gratitude (LOG), it makes sense to define this concept clearly. It's instructive to begin by listing the many things that an LOG is *not*.

- It isn't an email.

- It isn't a text.

- It isn't an emoji.

- It isn't a GIF.

- It isn't a TikTok.

- It isn't Snapchat.

- It isn't a DM.

- It isn't a mere thank-you note.

It is a *letter*, preferably sent by mail, but hand-delivered (placed on a bureau, on a desk, in a suitcase, or in a backpack, for example) is equally appropriate.

My personal preference is to type letters on plain or custom stationery. This spares the recipient the burden of attempting to decipher objectionable handwriting. More importantly, it provides a permanent archive of every letter written—what was said to whom, and when.

However—Letters of Gratitude can easily (and in many cases should) be handwritten, as that method offers a much more personal touch. (And in the majority of cases, the writer will only be sending a manageable or modest number of letters and is unlikely to be sending repeat or "encore letters" to the same individual or individuals, so the handwritten technique is an excellent option.)

A Letter of Gratitude differs from a run-of-the-mill thank-you note (not to imply that handwritten thank-you notes are run-of-the-mill anymore, not in the era in which we live) in one precise capacity: A typical thank-you note is sent for a specific reason or action.

Examples might include acknowledging a gift, a dinner invitation, a party, a meeting, or an introduction. The list goes on. But an LOG is showing gratitude for someone (or a couple, or a group) in general. This is the key difference.

A Letter of Gratitude is thanking someone just for being themselves. Not for any specific deed or action. Later in this book, there's a chapter titled "Ten Concepts to Jump-Start Letters of

Gratitude." One of the suggested techniques is to open a letter by thanking the recipient for something specific before segueing into a general discussion of why the writer is grateful to the recipient in the bigger picture. But the biggest difference between the thank-you note in comparison to the LOG is the deeper, wider, and more general sense of gratitude the person sending the letter feels, above and beyond any specific action.

Finally, the reason stationery, a stamp, and an envelope are preferential is that there's something almost ceremonial about receiving mail (that isn't junk mail, catalogs, bills, etc.) in the modern era. It shows that the sender, the person professing gratitude to the recipient, has taken the time, the extra effort, and the consideration to share their positive thoughts and feelings in a more permanent and meaningful manner.

3

Gratitude TIGER

It's a logical assumption that this book title and the website gratitudetiger.com are an homage, or in some manner have something to do with the iconic golfer Tiger Woods.

It's a rational conclusion, as I was deeply imbedded in the golf world for more than two decades, met the prodigy on a few occasions, wrote about him constantly through his prolonged dominant phase, and then continued to chronicle the many controversies after his fall from grace.

Furthermore, we both turned "pro" at nearly the same time. Tiger caught the world's attention by winning the Masters by a mind-boggling dozen shots in April 1997 (though technically he had given up his amateur status and turned professional the previous autumn). And as expressed elsewhere within this text, my debut as a golf columnist began on the first day of 1998. You could argue we "grew up together," professionally speaking. Though you couldn't argue the fact that, in regards to our parallel careers in golf, Tiger's was approximately one million times more successful!

However, this long association with golf, golf writing, the PGA Tour, and wonderment at the preternatural natural skills of Mr. Woods has absolutely zero to do with the name of this book or the eponymous website.

TIGER is simply an acronym:

- **T**apping
- **I**nto
- **G**ratitude
- **E**ngenders
- **R**ewards

TIGER is just a fancy way of saying it's better to give than to receive. When you *give* gratitude, regularly, liberally, and often, you *will* be rewarded for doing so.

Writing Letters of Gratitude (at least in this author's opinion) are the ultimate manifestation of this aforementioned "tapping." But thinking about gratitude, bringing it to the forefront of your thought process, and letting it seep into your consciousness on any and every occasion will help change your mindset, lead to a calmer demeanor, and ultimately reward you.

There's not always time, interest, or the wherewithal to write a letter. But there's always time to say "thank you," nod your head and smile, make a kind remark to the checkout person, offer a quick compliment to the person standing next to you—the list of innocuous pleasantries is endless. Just remember to give gratitude to everyone and every situation in which you find yourself. It's helpful, healing, and will add buoyancy to your mood, even for a heartbeat.

Speaking of heartbeats, this short chapter is in many ways the second, simpler, and more general "heartbeat" of this book (the primary one being "The Seven Pillars of Expressive Gratitude").

Just remember **TIGER**—Tapping into Gratitude Engenders Rewards.

(Besides, it makes for a catchy book title and website, wouldn't you agree?)

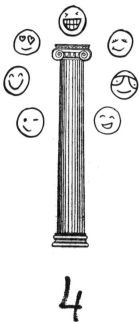

4

The Seven Pillars of Expressive Gratitude

Use your imagination for a moment and consider this entire volume to be a gourmet meal at a white linen restaurant. Every other chapter herein is just an accoutrement. They are the breadsticks, cocktails, the amuse-bouche, the salad, side dishes, wine, cheese course, dessert, coffee, and so on. But the thousand or so words following these two paragraphs are the main course, the entrée, the raison d'etre of the entire project. This is the heart of the whole matter.

The central theme of *Gratitude Tiger* is to urge readers to take on the hobby of writing Letters of Gratitude themselves. These seven pillars are the primary reasons why one should, and they are ultimately why this book exists.

1. Writing Letters of Gratitude makes the *letter writer* feel wonderful.

In many ways, this is the most important principle of this delightful hobby. You write the letters for yourself, first and foremost. You will receive three hits of dopamine with each letter you undertake. The first comes when you identify the recipient. The second comes when you review the completed letter. And the third comes when you put the letter in the mail.

There is a compelling reason why I've written nearly three hundred Letters of Gratitude, and it's not because I'm some sort of altruist or Mother Teresa–wannabe. First and foremost, these letters are created because they make me feel good.

It's a bit like helping an elderly individual or differently abled person cross a busy road. It's somewhat like offering precise directions to a frazzled passerby. It's like these things, but much, much more. Another paragraph or two could be devoted to drawing further analogies, but the readers (soon to be letter writers, one can only hope!) will have to experience the feeling of warmth and accomplishment for themselves.

The fact is that when writing that first letter, a week or so shy of Thanksgiving 2013, I had no inkling there would ever be a second letter, much less nearly 300 more. There's little more to be added, other than to say that the act of extending yourself, reaching out and showing deep gratitude to those in your orbit who have helped you, is an intoxicating experience. That's why it's been repeated over and over through the years.

2. A Letter of Gratitude makes the *recipient* feel wonderful.

This is the most self-apparent of the seven pillars, but there are two major points to be made.

The first is the fact that every human being is battling through life. For the fortunate few, it's often a minor skirmish. But for the mass of humanity, every day is all-out warfare. Trying to get ahead, stay ahead, scratch, claw, do whatever is necessary to survive, to fight on for another day. And into the midst of the daily travails comes a letter, completely unexpected, out of the blue. A familiar name from the recipient's past or present is in the return address area. And the gist of the communication is the writer emphasizing how grateful they are to know the recipient, how that person has made a difference in their lives, and how knowing or being associated with the recipient has been of benefit. This is going to make most people's day, if not their week!

The second point: Think about the contents of your daily mail. For most people, it's an unsavory combination of bills, circulars, commercial postcards, Val-Paks, political solicitations, catalogs, and detritus of every stripe. And one day, amid this daily dross, comes a letter. It's not your birthday, and it's not Christmas. And the contents contained within are singing (or perhaps just humming) your praises; the writer has taken the time to let you know you've been a valuable and important person in their lives. This is powerful, unforgettable stuff.

3. Receiving a Letter of Gratitude makes the recipient feel good *about the letter writer*.

Most people want to be liked. Plain and simple. Not everyone. Powerful CEO or board member types might prefer to be admired or respected. Despots, dictators, and authoritarian types might prefer to be feared. There are curmudgeons, misanthropes, malcontents, and hermits living high on a hillside who just don't give a fig about being liked, or even associating with the rest of us. But all these examples are exceptions, because the vast majority of humankind would prefer to be liked rather than disliked.

There are only three guarantees in life: death, taxes, and the recipient's opinion of the author of the Letter of Gratitude won't diminish. It might not necessarily go up, but the altruistic, giving nature of the hobby ensures that you will at the very least be held in the same regard as you were before the mailman delivered the goods. But the odds are great that from that day forward the recipient will hold you in higher esteem.

4. It's a creative process.

It doesn't matter if you're a novelist, screenwriter, poet, or sculptor. Everyone needs more creativity in their lives. The act of writing a Letter of Gratitude, no matter the length, the detail, or the complexity is at its essence a creative process.

5. It turns your focus *outward*.

Five simple words describe most of humanity: "What's in it for me?" What's in it for *my* family, *my* friend group, *my* company, *my* organization? When you are engaged in writing a Letter of Gratitude, your focus, for the ten, twenty, or thirty minutes it takes you to compose your thoughts and put them on paper, is on *the other person.* The self-involved nature that permeates our personalities is sublimated during the time it takes to write, and that is a very healthy way to be.

6. There is a "ripple effect."

Suppose you decide to write a letter to your old college roommate. You've been out of touch for fifteen years, but you decide to rock her world and reach out in this uniquely delightful manner. You reminisce about sorority hijinks, the way she got you through trigonometry class, that crazy spring break your junior year, whatever. You tell her how grateful you are for this long-standing friendship.

She is so taken aback by this out-of-the-blue, heartfelt communique that *she* decides to pay it forward. She thinks: *My cousin Janie was like a sister to me for nearly a decade; we were inseparable up at our grandparents' lake house every summer from the time we were ten until we went off to college. But I haven't even spoken to her since the last family reunion. I'm going to write* her *a letter!* Thus, the ripple effect ensues.

7. There is a legacy effect.

Only two things can transpire after you write a Letter of Gratitude: The recipient will pass away prior to the letter writer, or the letter writer will pass away before the recipient.

Of my hundreds of letters, more than a dozen were sent to individuals who have subsequently passed. Some were of natural causes, as they might have been elderly relatives or mentors. Others were terminally ill, facing their looming mortality, and they were written to with a sense of urgency, telling them I'd been grateful to know them and gently suggesting to them, despite their dire circumstances, to be grateful for the lives they'd lived, the families they'd produced, their legacies, accomplishments, triumphs, and so on.

When word arrived that someone I'd previously written to had died, the first thought that came to my mind was how thankful I was that I'd reached out to them, sharing my feelings with them while they were still around to receive them. As is said elsewhere in this book, Ralph Waldo Emerson's words never ring truer than in these circumstances: "You can never do a kindness too soon, because you never know how soon it will be too late."

On the other side of the coin, regarding *the letter writer* passing away before the *recipient,* thankfully I have no personal experience in this regard! However, when that day comes, my hope is that that as word spreads and individuals in my orbit get the news, they'll think, *He threw me for a loop some years ago with this completely unexpected letter expressing gratitude for our relationship. I'm sorry to hear this news.*

One can only hope, anyway.

5

Proactive versus Reactive Gratitude

Here's the bottom line: Every human being on the planet—it doesn't matter how brutal their circumstance, how untenable their situation, or how difficult life might be—has moments when they feel *reactive* gratitude. This is adrenaline-fueled gratitude, reflexive gratitude, gratitude-by-Pavlov.

This isn't learned or practiced behavior; it occurs as naturally as an eyeblink, a sneeze, or a peal of laughter. By contrast, *proactive* gratitude is something else entirely. It's when you make the conscious decision to find a heartbeat of gratitude in any given circumstance. You take a moment or two and reflect on the goodness of a situation and then continue with your day. A notable difference between reactive and proactive gratitude is that the former lasts longer, has a bit more permanence, and, for lack of a better term, "hits harder."

However, learning to be proactively grateful, embracing that gratitude mindset, is beneficial for emotional well-being and a positive mindset. It's like getting a tiny shot of dopamine every time you make the choice to be grateful in that moment.

Moments of reactive gratitude are fewer and further between than moments of proactive gratitude, which is something you need to conjure. After all, how often do you win the lottery? (Reactive gratitude at its finest!) To illustrate, here are fifteen examples of reactive gratitude, followed by more than twice as many examples of proactive gratitude. Just another little exercise in helping the reader develop that valuable gratitude mindset.

Fifteen examples of reactive gratitude:

- Upon receiving a benign medical diagnosis after having cause for concern

- When your turbulent, white-knuckle flight lands safely

- When your spouse narrowly avoids a multicar pileup on the interstate

- When your child or grandchild gets admitted into their college of choice

- When you avoid yet another round of layoffs at your company

- When your kid makes the varsity team, or, even better, is named captain

- When the auto mechanic tells you it's going to be a simple, inexpensive fix

- When you beat out the other qualified candidates for the work promotion

- When you're headed in the opposite direction on the grid-locked highway

- When your child or grandchild is born healthy and thriving

- When your son or daughter returns safely after a military deployment

- When a passerby pulls over to help you change a flat tire on a busy road

- When you're the guest of honor at a surprise party

- When a missing pet returns home (or is returned) safely

- When your elderly parent or grandparent pulls through after a health scare

Thirty-one examples of proactive gratitude:

- Listening to birdsong

- Admiring autumn leaves

- Finishing a jigsaw or crossword puzzle

- Enjoying the quietude of a snowfall

- When a song you love but haven't heard in ages comes on the radio
- Getting your car washed
- Watching kids play
- Deer springing and bouncing through a meadow
- Finishing a home improvement project
- Completing a road race
- Building a treehouse (or cabinet, patio, or model airplane)
- Planting a garden
- Harvesting a few vegetables from that garden
- Running into an old friend
- Finding the right size and color on the sale rack
- When the grandkids conk out
- Cooking your spouse their favorite breakfast
- Visiting or calling an elderly relative or neighbor
- Bringing your favorite dish to a potluck
- Listening to an enlightening lecture
- Finishing a good book (or movie or miniseries)
- Being asked for your advice
- When the server brings you a free dessert
- Watching fireworks

- Viewing the sunrise or sunset

- Seeing a rainbow

- Enjoying a hearty laugh

- Providing precise directions to a confused passerby

- Making it inside just before the deluge begins

- Pulling up to the fuel pump just as the person ahead of you drives away

- When the person with eight or ten grocery items lets you pay for your milk and bananas (or twelve-pack and Doritos—no judgment!) ahead of them

In conclusion, almost every opportunity or circumstance (outside of a splinter, stubbed toe, wasp sting, pink slip, or flight cancellation) might be a moment to feel a quick pulse of proactive gratitude. Keep it in the forefront of your mind, try and see the positive in any neutral or negative situation, and work to develop your capacity for proactive gratitude. It's a game-changer and can lead to improved emotional well-being and greater equanimity.

6

Obligation versus Compulsion

More than fifty years ago, I was obligated to write thank-you notes, and not just a few.

I had a bar mitzvah in November 1973, shortly after turning thirteen. (This is a mainstay of the Jewish religion, a ritual signifying passage into "adulthood." Although for the vast majority, present company included, it takes at least another decade, maybe two, to really get the hang of things!) My ceremony was witnessed by one hundred and something attendees. It was a smattering of my classmates and neighborhood chums, but mostly friends of my parents. (Perhaps it was several hundred people. It's now too far in the rearview mirror, and nobody's left to recall the guest list accurately.)

My parents were sticklers for thank-you notes, and thus I was tasked with writing to each and every gift-giver of a savings bond, sweater, scarf, personal check, pen set, prayer book, or gewgaw that ended up on our doorstep or in the mailbox. (Brief aside: One artifact improbably remains from those ancient boyhood days—a Nixon-era pair of binoculars, still useful, still at the ready, stored in our front hall closet. Though no guess will be forthcoming as to who bequeathed this durable precision instrument, I applaud their foresight and gift-giving acumen!)

All of this is to say that many, if not most, thank-you notes are, at least in part, an obligation. (Unless they're not. I have given wedding gifts, for example, and never received an acknowledgment. Most anyone reading these words has suffered a similar fate.)

Modern manners (or lack thereof) aside, if you were raised a certain way, a handwritten note of thanks was expected. It's just what you offered in return for a dinner invite, a gift, a party, or a festive gathering. In my opinion, it's far more meaningful and thoughtful than a follow-up phone call or text, which, let's face it, serves the exact same purpose.

Times have changed, and written notes of thanks are mostly going the way of Blu-Ray Discs and charcoal briquettes. Although there will always be throwbacks, who then teach their kids to be throwbacks, so the ancient art of envelope and stamp will continue onward, albeit in a state of diminution.

Here's the gist: This is a book about Letters of Gratitude. Not thank-you notes. And at the risk of getting into the weeds for just a few paragraphs, there's a big difference.

Oftentimes, unless it's been a humdinger of a party, or the gift you received knocked your socks off, or the dinner thrown in your honor brought you to the verge of tears, a thank-you note is some-what of an obligation.

By contrast, Letters of Gratitude should be more of a compulsion. If you feel strongly enough about someone that you want to reach out and share your deep gratitude to them, letting them know the positive impact they've had on your life, this is miles beyond any obligation.

Furthermore, a gift-giver, party-thrower, or dinner host might be expecting some sort of thanks, be it a digital or Luddite version, for their generosity. But because LOGs are by nature unexpected, the word *obligation* doesn't factor into the equation. They (almost always) come as a complete surprise to the recipient, which obviates any pressure or expectation on the writer.

As has been stated repeatedly throughout these pages, my organic understanding of gratitude is due solely to the fact that I've created and mailed literally hundreds of letters. Not once has a letter been written out of any sense of obligation. I've never thought, "Bill got a letter recently, and he might've mentioned it to our mutual friend Steve, so perhaps I need to write to Steve also." Nothing of the sort.

This has been a highly personal hobby, and the purpose of this book is to encourage others to consider taking up this highly personal hobby themselves. And to get even more personal, all these letters, for lack of a better term, *bubble up* from my core. I identify who to write to, whether it's an impulsive letter that needs to be written ASAP, or someone who's been on the "to-do" list for a while. Either way, feelings of goodwill and gratitude flow like hot lava.

Not everyone is so effusive, and perhaps these words of affection, respect, and admiration don't come so easily. Not to worry. There's cogent advice for the taciturn reader (and writer) a bit later in the chapter titled "Seven Paragraphs, Seven Sentences, Seven Words."

Furthermore, it's not what you say or how you say it. It's the fact that you said it in the first place. Maya Angelou summed it up beautifully. The essayist and poet is widely quoted as saying, "I've learned that people will forget what you said, people will forget what you did, but people will never forget how you made them feel."

Write a Letter of Gratitude and make the recipient feel terrific. Don't do it out of obligation. Do it out of compulsion. And when you're finished, odds are you will feel terrific, too.

7

Alternative Gratitude Practices—No Postage Required

"**W**ith great effort comes great gratification." These are the wise words of a Canadian named Stephanie Pearl-McPhee, known to her fans, no kidding, as the "Yarn Harlot." (Apparently, she's some kind of knitting guru.)

It's my personal belief that writing Letters of Gratitude doesn't necessarily require "great" effort, though they take a bit of doing. I agree wholeheartedly with her second point, because these letters do provide great gratification. But effective letter writing is a learned and practiced skill and isn't everyone's forte.

This chapter will outline a trio of alternative gratitude practices you can try on for size, none of which require adept communication skills, second or third drafts, an envelope, or a trip to the mailbox. These aren't technically examples of expressive gratitude, which is the gold standard, but they do provide a gratitude mindset, which is undoubtedly a step in the right direction.

- **The Gratitude Journal.** This concept requires scant explanation, particularly for anyone reading this book! For the very few who might be uninitiated, the journal is either a notebook or diary where one jots down random thoughts of gratitude on a regular, preferably daily, basis. In lieu of that, at least two or three times a week. The key element is to be sure to date each entry!

  If you run into an old friend and have an unexpected catch-up session, that's worth an entry. A tasty lunch at a restaurant you've never visited previously, an unexpected A grade for your math-phobic daughter—there are an uncountable number of reasons to be grateful on any given day.

  But if you don't record them and date them, they'll quickly recede into the misty haze of memory. So, record dutifully, and check back on your entries every week or a few times a month. You'll be delighted (or at least pleased) to recall these little moments of grace that otherwise might've disappeared into the ether.

- **The Gratitude Jar.** This is virtually identical to the journal, but with a slight twist. Instead of a piggy bank and coins, you have a glass jar (or similar receptacle) and a stack of index cards.

  Write down thoughts of gratitude, minor moments that made you smile or happy, and so on, on the index cards.

Once again, be sure to date each entry. Once a week, a few times monthly, or whenever the jar starts to fill up, empty the contents. Reread these things that made you glad or grateful and when they occurred. Just like with the journal, you'll be reminded of things you might've forgotten had you not taken a few moments to record them.

- **Count Your Blessings.** Literally. While a journal or a jar aren't tools of my choosing, this is a mandatory two-minute exercise in self-reflection conducted every evening after crawling into bed.

   Here's how it works: As you're settling down, after adjusting the covers, the pillow, and so on, silently recall everything that provided a moment's pleasure or a flash of gratitude, no matter how trivial, that happened that day. Do it chronologically, from morning until evening, so nothing slips through the cracks.

Here's a typical stream of consciousness that illustrates the concept: *Glad to have had yogurt and fruit for breakfast, even though it was tempting to polish off the extra pancakes the kids didn't eat. It was a nice surprise to see Steve at the hardware store; haven't run into him in months. It was perfect timing that the car ahead of me at the gas station pulled out at the exact moment that I pulled up to the pump. My colleagues did a good job touching up the finer points of our work presentation. Thankfully the Zoom conference only lasted thirty minutes when they had allotted an hour. Glad cousin Jason was in town on business, but still had time to join us for dinner.* And on and on and on.

Recall every pleasant conversation, streak of consecutive green lights, unexpected text exchange, highlight of every meal, if your team won, an enlightening news article or podcast, something amusing your kid or grandkid said or did—every little thing from morning until night. This "recollection reverie" will help flick the "off switch" on your nervous system, hopefully have a calming effect, and allow you to fall asleep more easily.

It's a simple, enjoyable, effortless way to improve both your gratitude mindset and initiate the process for a restful (as opposed to restless) slumber. As you get more adept and tuned in to recalling the sweet minutia of the day, you might be surprised that your recollection of pleasant interludes stretches to twenty or thirty separate instances!

8

The Health Benefits
of Fierce Gratitude

As evidenced by the opening sentence in the opening chapter, this book is a personal journey. It details an unusual, inadvertent transmogrification from a regular Joe into someone who became, out of happenstance, deeply invested in gratitude.

The desire is that the reader, hopefully intrigued by the concept of embracing proactive, expressive gratitude, and all its ancillary benefits, will hop on board themselves. If they're not quite ready to purchase a ticket on my personal letter-writing freight train, perhaps they'll test the waters with their own gratitude choo-choo, or, at the very least, a handcar.

That said, and personal journey notwithstanding, there are a couple of chapters within these pages that require some facts, figures, and statistics to bolster the argument. One of these instances is the chapter following this one, which discusses gratitude in the workplace. This is another.

A sage podcast host once remarked that it's hard to be angry, scared, or resentful when you're grateful. I agreed to a point but offered the caveat that it's hard to have these conflicting emotions *concurrently*. There's plenty of room in the human psyche for a wide range of emotions, both negative and positive, and feelings of all stripes are constantly jostling for position in our mind.

What's inarguable is that gratitude is good for the mind and body in many ways. No need to belabor this point simply because you can doom-scroll (perhaps the more apt description is delight-scroll) on the internet for untold hours and find example after example of how gratitude is beneficial.

Let's hit a couple of major points before going deeper on just a few.

A wide range of research shows that living a gratitude-centric life can:

- Lower blood pressure

- Increase equanimity

- Improve sleep patterns

- Enhance overall well-being

Those might be considered the "Big Four Benefits," and they are certainly among the major building blocks when discussing the many benefits of proactive gratitude. But the American Heart Association takes it several steps further. Their research shows that focusing on gratitude can also improve mood, increase immunity, and decrease depression, anxiety, chronic pain, and disease.[2]

Psychology Today, a magazine that will soon be celebrating its sixtieth anniversary, contends that focused gratitude can enhance empathy, generosity, self-esteem, and mental strength, while reducing aggression.[3]

The *Journal of the American Medical Association*, known as *JAMA*, recently released results of a fascinating study linking gratitude to longevity.[4] You could get so deep in the weeds with this one you'd need to be ambidextrous with both a scythe and a sickle to come up for air. But the gist of it is this: A study of nearly fifty thousand older women (a population of nurses) answered six questions relating to their feelings of gratitude back in 2016. On a 1 (strongly disagree) to 7 (strongly agree) scale, they responded to questions such as:

"I have so much in my life to be thankful for."

"If I had to list everything that I felt grateful for, it would be a very long list."

"I am grateful to a wide variety of people."

"Long amounts of time can go by before I feel grateful to something/someone."

The study took into consideration wellness routines such as diet and exercise, the nurse's habits regarding smoking and drinking alcohol, and history of health issues like heart disease, cancer,

2   American Heart Association editorial staff, December 18, 2023, Heart.org/healthy-living.

3   Ross E. O'Hara, PhD, "The Power of Gratitude," November 2, 2022, *Psychology Today*, https://www.psychologytoday.com/us/blog/nudging-ahead/202211/the-power-of-gratitude.

4   Ying Chen, ScD, Olivia I. Okereke, MD, SM, Eric S. Kim, PhD, et al, "Gratitude and Mortality Among Older US Female Nurses," July 3, 2024, Jama Network, https://jamanetwork.com/journals/jamapsychiatry/fullarticle/2820770.

and diabetes. The findings illustrated that the risk of dying over the next three years was *significantly lower* for those who felt more gratitude for their lives. Depending on the health/wellness factors, the difference was anywhere from 29 to 21 percent less for those who focused on gratitude.

Greater Good Magazine, named after the eponymous science center at the University of California at Berkeley, considered by the prestigious *Utne Reader* to be among the top independent publications in the nation, offers further findings. Their research shows that focusing on gratitude can assist in blocking toxic emotions such as envy, resentment, regret, fear, and depression.

Most interestingly, and keeping with the theme of this book, the publication funded a unique research study involving three hundred volunteers, predominantly college students, who were reporting mental health challenges and seeking counseling help at their university. The researchers, Joel Wong and Joshua Brown, are both PhDs and professors at the University of Indiana. The duo reported that within the larger body of volunteers, the focus group that had been assigned to write three letters of gratitude over three weeks reported significantly improved mental health within a month or so after completing their letter-writing assignments.[5]

The mind-blowing part is that after creating the letters, most of these volunteers chose not to mail or deliver them! Yet just the act of writing them had a positive effect on their mental health.

Honestly, and as an aside, this little factoid is borderline incomprehensible. Take the time and effort to write a letter and then choose not to deliver it to the person you've earmarked? Might

---

5   Joel Wong and Joshua Brown, "How Gratitude Changes You and Your Brain," June 6, 2017, *Greater Good Magazine*, https://greatergood.berkeley.edu/article/item/how_gratitude_changes_you_and_your_brain.

as well order a pizza, pay the delivery person, and then just let it sit on the counter until it's cold and congealed. Or travel to Paris and make the conscious decision to never glance upward toward the Eiffel Tower.

It's not easy, as the saying goes, to "walk a mile in another person's moccasins." But if someone has difficulty sharing feelings, has some repression issues, is afraid to feel vulnerable, and doesn't like to, for lack of a better term, "go deep," then what many might consider peculiar behavior is somehow normal. But offering a guess in advance of these findings, I would have thought perhaps only one in four would be reluctant to send the letter they've written, not one in four willing to send the letter. The moral is that you learn something new every day!

In conclusion, you can check out any magazine or online platform you care to, from *American Spectator* to *Yoga Journal*. (There are no publications beginning with Z that most people have heard of.) You will discover findings similar to what's detailed in the preceding pages. It can be sliced, diced, chopped, and minced any way you care to examine it.

Gratitude is an incredibly positive attribute to possess. And proactive, expressive gratitude is best of all.

9

How Fierce Gratitude Can Enhance Corporate Culture

Horrible Bosses is a 2011 black comedy with an all-star cast including Jason Bateman, Jason Sudeikis, Jennifer Aniston, Jamie Foxx, and Kevin Spacey. Though the film's budget was less than $40,000,000, it grossed more than five times that amount, north of $200,000,000 at the box office. In theory, this means that millions of moviegoers could relate to the subject matter.

Most workers wouldn't necessarily refer to their bosses as *horrible* per se. But perhaps adjectives such as *aloof, disinterested, self-centered, humorless, autocratic, self-involved, eccentric, difficult,* and *demanding* might pepper the conversation. There's a simple method for bosses to maintain cordial, even amiable, relationships with their charges. All it takes is a little gratitude. But before we go there, here are some easily digestible workplace facts and figures:

According to Gallup polling, millennials and Gen Z (born between 1980—2001) now make up nearly half of the full-time workforce in the United States. Their research shows that the *top priority* of these youngish workers is an employer concerned with their employees' well-being. A recent Gallup survey of 67,000 workers of *all ages* shows that more than two-thirds aren't engaged with their work, a number that has increased appreciably in this decade. Fully half of all workers are not opposed to changing jobs, underscoring the fact that employee retention is one of the costliest, immediate, and most vexing problems that employers face.[6]

Deloitte is a famed multinational accounting firm with nearly a half million employees worldwide. Their 2024 survey, the thirteenth conducted by the firm, reached some 23,000 Gen Zs and millennials in forty-four countries.

According to Deloitte, in terms of workplace stress, more than half of millennials and Gen Z employees cite that *not being recognized* and/or rewarded for their efforts is their single biggest concern. This is slightly higher than other stressors named such as long hours or feeling their work has little meaning or purpose. Furthermore, salary and other financial benefits only factored in about 20 percent of survey responses regarding why they chose their current employers.[7]

Research of this nature is readily available, and statistics could be spewed for a dozen more pages. But the long and short of it is that compensation is no longer the primary driver of workplace satisfaction. Being recognized and appreciated by one's bosses and

---

6   Ryan Pendell and Sara Vander Helm, "Generation Disconnected: Data on Gen Z in the Workplace," November 11, 2022, Gallup.com/Workplace.

7   Deloitte 2024 Gen Z and Millennial Survey: Living and Working with Purpose in a Transforming World, deloitte.com, https://www2.deloitte.com/content/dam/Deloitte/at/Documents/presse/at-deloitte-global-gen-z-millennial-survey-gesamte-studie.pdf.

superiors has taken precedence as baby boomers exit stage left, and younger generations move up the employment ladder.

This research is fascinating, because other than Peace Corps volunteers, guidance counselors, and full-time poets (not to mention cops, teachers, and firemen), most workers of my generation were money motivated. Initial queries regarding a potential job had to do with starting salary, potential for bonuses, room for advancement, and amount of vacation time. The only compensation for time and effort expended on the job was compensation. Everything else was secondary, tertiary, or mostly irrelevant.

However, there are many industries where major salary bumps, bonuses, stock options, and other capitalist tools are simply unavailable. Consider the beautiful mountain hamlet of Park City, Utah, where we make our home. The fuel that keeps this economic engine purring is tourism—specifically, ski resorts, restaurants, and lodging components. For the sake of brevity, the focus will remain on skiing, but the other industries are similar.

If you choose to spend five months a year in ski boots, wearing a distinctive winter uniform, assisting guests in whatever form that takes, you're not in it to get rich. It's a lifestyle choice, attracting those who love the outdoors, the mountains, the alpine setting, and being around similarly inclined, dynamic, service-oriented colleagues. Salaries are modest, bonuses (beyond a Starbucks gift card) are nonexistent, and while there are perks (a ski pass!), nobody outside of the C-suite is amassing a fortune or even fattening their 401(k).

So in lieu of traditional methods (i.e., raises) available to show appreciation to valued employees, how can a boss keep morale high and engender employee loyalty? Gratitude is one simple answer. It can go a long, long way.

It doesn't matter if you're a branch manager, a small business owner, or in charge of a department, division, or area. You can have four employees under your auspices or four thousand. To be most effective in the role of employer or supervisor, you *must* take the time, be it weekly, monthly, semiannually, or whenever it's deserved, to offer praise and bestow gratitude to your people.

The thrust of this book is to urge readers to develop the skills to wax rhapsodic to those who have helped along life's journey with Letters of Gratitude. However, in this case, it's perfectly fine to be brief and to the point. Suffice it to say a boss can offer direct praise to an employee with an economy of words.

Time is limited in the work environment, and if one makes a point of showing gratitude to one dozen (or one hundred) employees simultaneously (around the holidays, for example), it will be hard to differentiate one letter (or note) from the next. Although *writing* a note is ideal, in this instance, it's not a breach to use email, direct messaging, text, Slack, or any other preferred form of digital communication.

This isn't about the "grand gesture," the company-wide speech, the bouquet of roses, the framed commendation, the breakroom cake party, and so on. It's just the idea of regular or occasional words of praise directed toward those who are doing a good job and those in need of a micro-morale boost.

One last point: It's most effective to use praise with no other agenda, not in combination with anything else. Don't tack a complimentary sentence or paragraph onto a request, a new deadline, or a status report. Just offer gratitude by itself, whether written or spoken, for maximum effect.

As the one who must keep the ship afloat and moving forward, keeping the department profitable, maintaining order, doling out assignments, and making sure the work gets done, bosses by nature aren't in position to win popularity contests. You can be a perfectionist, a nitpicker, a taskmaster, and a workaholic. But if you regularly make a point to express gratitude to your charges, verbally or by written word or deed, chances are greatly increased that none will consider you a "horrible boss."

10

Seven Paragraphs, Seven Sentences, Seven Words

On the first day of fourth or fifth grade, your teacher might have given you a writing assignment titled "My Summer Vacation." She most likely insisted that this essay be one hundred words in length. This is a daunting project for many nine- or ten-year-olds.

Let's be a fly on the wall as little Johnny labors to complete this task:

"I went to camp." (Four words down, ninety-six to go.) "It was fun." (Ninety-three to go.) "It was hot." (Ninety to go.) "I played basketball and volleyball." (Eighty-five left!) "I also went swimming." (Eighty-one left.) "The food wasn't good." (Seventy-seven left! *This is impossible!*)

"My bunkmates were Steve, Joey, Morgan, and Lance." (Sixty-nine left.) "Lance smelled funny." (Sixty-six left. *This is torture.*) "Our counselor was Ivan." (Sixty-two words left. *I'll never finish this!*)

As you might've surmised by reading *Gratitude Tiger* to this point, this type of writing assignment wasn't an impediment for yours truly. Call it what you will—verbosity, effusiveness, gift of gab, whatever—even as a grade schooler, I'm sure it took me at least one hundred words just to clear my throat!

Writing Letters of Gratitude follows a similar trajectory. My letters are typed, full-page, freewheeling streams of consciousness. Filling the entire sheet of stationery is almost never an issue. Far more often the typeface needs to be shrunk from 14 to 12, occasionally down to 11, to fit it all in. For example, in 2024 alone, various letters written and sent have obliquely referenced Barry Manilow, Tony Soprano, Bill Withers, Vito Corleone, and The Hollies!

Not everyone is wired like this. (Thank goodness for small mercies.) Many or most individuals have more of a filter that for no explicable reason is simply MIA from my DNA.

Not to worry. You can still write effective, powerful, moving, memorable, and impactful Letters of Gratitude using an economy of words. Just because it suits me to natter on for seven or eight paragraphs doesn't mean you can't accomplish the same thing in seven or eight sentences. Or even seven or eight words.

There will be no belaboring of the "seven sentences" concept—just two hypothetical examples: one to a friend, and one in a work context. Suffice it to say that a seven-sentence note is a very thoughtful and all-encompassing gesture. (Particularly when an etiquette authority like Emily Post claims that four or five sentences are perfectly adequate for expressing written thanks.)

A Seven-Sentence Letter of Gratitude to a Friend:

Dear Bill,

This note will take you by surprise, but I wanted to share my deep gratitude with you. When we first met all those years ago as lifeguards at the YMCA, I wasn't sure we would ever hit it off. But I must say, my worries were unfounded! From our college days until now, you've been a great friend to me, and I wanted to thank you for being such a welcome presence in my life. I'm glad that we still spend time together, even thirty years after graduation. Furthermore, I'm pleased that Chloe and Anne have become so friendly also. Our little gang of four has enjoyed plenty of fun times together in recent years, and I'm sure we'll have many more in the future!

A Seven-Sentence Letter of Gratitude in a Work Context:

Dear Eliza,

I just wanted to take a moment and "officially" thank you for my recent promotion! I've admired your work ethic and acumen since I came on board three years ago. Part of the success that's come my way is because I've modeled myself after your example. The fact that you chose me over the other qualified candidates to lead the new division is a tremendous confidence boost. I will do my very best to reward your faith in my abilities. There will be a learning curve as I dive in, so please don't be surprised when I need to ask questions or bounce ideas off you. But I want to express my sincere gratitude and will approach these expanded duties with energy and enthusiasm.

Now we'll examine what at first glance might appear to be the tricky part. But judge for yourself. Here are seven examples of seven (or eight!)-word Notes of Gratitude—it's not easy to categorize a single sentence as a bona fide letter—that will be offered for examination in three distinct categories: to a friend, to a loved one, and within a work context.

Seven-Word Notes of Gratitude to a Friend:

- I couldn't have done it without you!
- They broke the mold with you. Thanks!
- My dear friend, you are absolute aces!
- I cannot thank you enough for your help.
- I never thought we'd pull it off!
- What a wonderful time we had! Thank you!
- I'm incredibly grateful you offered a hand.

Seven-Word Notes of Gratitude to a Loved One:

- You absolutely mean the world to me.

- I lucked out in the daughter department!

- You are such a wonderful big brother.

- This family is lucky to have you.

- I love you and cherish your presence.

- I'm beyond grateful that you're my husband.

- Marrying you was my greatest decision ever.

Seven-Word Notes of Gratitude in a Work Context:

- You are THE cog in this machine!

- This department would cease functioning without you.

- What a fantastic job you are doing!

- Keep up the great work; it's inspiring.

- I'm so grateful we recruited you last year!

- I can't remember hearing a better presentation.

- This company is lucky to have you.

So, the long (seven paragraphs) and short (seven words) of it is this: Length isn't necessarily the determining factor regarding the effectiveness of a Letter (or Note) of Gratitude. Depth of feeling and zeal can be conveyed in an abbreviated fashion.

There's a certain luxury to unfurling sentences and paragraphs as one sees fit. But as little Johnny showcased at this chapter's outset, not everyone can riff or improvise on the page. Some people just don't have the bandwidth, inclination, or time to wax rhapsodically.

If that's the case, something short, sweet, heartfelt, pithy, and to the point is a wonderful substitute.

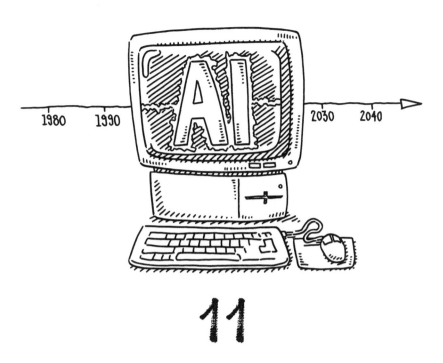

11

AI? Aye-Yai-Yai!

Suffering and celebrating were the two contrasting states of affairs (sadly, more of the former than latter) during dozens of launch parties and prearranged signing events at bookstores during the decades when golf writing was my chosen profession.

The launch parties were much preferred, reveling in the celebratory atmosphere of a new title just added to the oeuvre. These were festive affairs, usually well attended, sometimes with live music and libations, and often surrounded by family, friends, well-wishers, neighbors, innocent bystanders, or run-of-the-mill golf fanatics, many eagerly wielding their credit cards. The fat stack of gleaming new hardcovers as the event commenced diminished in height and girth as the evening wore on. Those occasions, fewer and further between, were heady times. The standard bookstore events? Not so much.

One (non) occasion that comes to mind, despite the fact it occurred more than two decades ago, was held at Harbour Town. Located at the southern tip of Hilton Head, South Carolina, it's far and away the best-known enclave on this enduringly popular resort island. I was ensconced in a touristy bookstore, as lonely as a lighthouse keeper. Ironic, because the iconic, candy-striped lighthouse, easily the best-known symbol of the island, was a five-minute walk from this all-but-deserted retail shop!

All by my lonesome, the Maytag Repairman come to life (a reference presumably lost on anyone born after 1990), and *finally*, in walks a customer. The sad irony? He had a copy of my brand-new book (my debut effort, released in 2003) under his arm already!

Imagine the chagrin of the proprietor. She spent a few bucks (probably very few, in retrospect) to advertise and promote this little shindig, and practically the only fellow walking through the door was already carrying the item she had hoped to sell! I wanted to cry but instead decided to laugh as he walked up to me to register a complaint, comment, or question about the book's contents.

We quickly started conversing about other matters, and within five minutes discovered an astonishing amount of common ground. Both Massachusetts natives, ties to New Hampshire's Lake Winnipesaukee, preoccupation with golf, fans of the Red Sox, wiseass senses of humor, sarcastic demeanors, cultural commonalities . . . the list goes on.

Long story short, there were very few books sold that day, but a friendship was born. Let's call him Marc. Over the past twenty years, Marc has accommodated me repeatedly. He's an ideal combination of generous, well-connected, and successful. Consequently, he's hosted me in South Carolina, Massachusetts, New Hampshire, and California. It's hard to reciprocate because he doesn't venture toward me, but I wander in his direction annually, if not more often, and he is a consistently generous, delightful host.

So, with this two-page preamble complete, the reader might be thinking, *What does this have to do with gratitude or gratitude letters?* Here's the gist: Marc remains unconvinced. He's a nonbeliever. More than once, he has said, "Saying thank you is enough. Make a call, send an email, or even a text. You don't have to go overboard."

He and his lovely wife, Deb, eventually received an LOG (late April 2021, if you're keeping score at home) some eighteen years after our initial encounter. He told me he appreciated the gesture very much, and there was no reason to doubt him.

However, on a recent visit to his bungalow in the California desert, he started opining on the wonders of artificial intelligence. He said, "You don't have to write letters. Watch this." He pulled out his iPhone, went to ChatGPT, and said, "Write a letter of gratitude to Joel Zuckerman, the former golf writer based in Park City, Utah." Ten seconds later there was a long, saccharine, overwrought ode to my writing ability, general good guy–ness, and a surfeit of schmaltz that would've resulted in a diabetic coma had it been read to conclusion.

I replied, "That's like the sappiest Hallmark card ever created. It needs to be edgier, with some snark." Marc wasted no time; he instructed the AI behemoth to do it again, with a healthy dose of sarcasm tossed in. Admittedly the second iteration, again produced in ten seconds, was a little better. Not as cloying, not so syrupy, but still missing something. Perhaps the human touch?

This analogy didn't come to mind then and there with my good friend and benefactor, but it's appropriate within this context.

Let's say you're a gourmet-level chef. Whether you learned from your grandmother, studied the culinary arts, ran the line at a top-end restaurant, no matter. You know how to slice and dice, flambe, and fricassee, the whole shebang.

You're hosting friends for a dinner party that evening, and your day goes completely sideways. As the afternoon slips away, the hour grows late, and you have no choice but to patronize the local chichi gourmet market. You fill your cart with delectable sides and a savory main dish, hot from the display case. You rush home, arrange it on your finest dishware, toss on the obligatory sprigs of parsley, and everyone digs in. They have a great time, the food is first-rate, and you deflect a slew of compliments from your impressed and satiated guests.

But the fact is, putting it plainly, you're a fraud. You employed no creativity, nor did you put your talents to use. All you did was select, purchase, plate, and garnish *someone else's work*.

An AI-generated Letter of Gratitude couldn't be more similar. Of course, you can fiddle with AI, or ChatGPT, and the letter recipient will be touched, perhaps overwhelmed by the gesture, and likely be none the wiser. But *you'll know*.

If you want to go that route, you might as well buy a pre-printed, mushy card by Hallmark, Blue Mountain, or American Greetings and just sign your name. (No different than Aunt Edna did for you every Christmas when she enclosed that five-dollar bill.)

Regarding doing it yourself, you don't need to be a wordsmith or uncommonly adept with the language arts. Something simple, straightforward, and from the heart will do.

Let's hammer this point home more comprehensively. Remember, the first pillar of gratitude is that writing LOGs will make *you, the writer,* feel good. The second pillar is that it makes *the recipient* feel good. An AI crutch fulfills the second pillar. But there's a reason it's the secondary and not the primary pillar! The essential reason to write these endearing, enriching letters is first and foremost for *yourself.* An AI-assisted letter is like riding a bicycle with training wheels. You're riding. But not really.

This is not to suggest that AI can't help a bit, maybe provide an idea or a train of thought, a turn of phrase, or a jumping-off point. But to completely rely on high-tech wizardry for what at its essence is a low-tech, feelings-based endeavor? Only two words come to mind: *amateur hour.*

12

Acknowledge You (Probably) Won't Be Acknowledged

One of my many questionable personality traits is the predilection for using ten-dollar words when a five-dollar word would easily fill the bill. (See, I just did it. *Tendency* or *preference* could have easily substituted for *predilection*. Perhaps it's because attention was hard to come by when I was a child.)

Here's a word that even the most erudite (did it again!) reader will likely find unfamiliar: *doxophobia*. It means the fear (or at the very least discomfort) of being praised. Doxophobia is more prevalent in society than you might think, and I can provide some empirical evidence.

Of the nearly three hundred Letters of Gratitude written and sent, approximately eighty, or what amounts to less than one-third, have been acknowledged by the recipient. There were a few return letters written, and the rest of the responses were calls, texts, or emails. However, about two out of every three recipients said nothing.

Truth be told, this used to be an irritation, if for no other reason than the inherent uncertainty that the letter had actually made its way to the intended target. (As an aside, the post office has a delivery success rate of slightly more than 99 percent, so using that math, it stands to reason that at least a couple of letters never reached their destination. More's the pity.)

Over time, I've learned to enjoy the process more than the result. In other words, the actual writing of the letters and sharing of the gratitude are the driving force. What happens after delivery and receipt are beyond my control. But this wasn't an easy lesson to learn, and even now there might be the occasional pang (just a beat) of ill feeling when a letter isn't acknowledged. However, the thrust of this chapter is to state definitively that even when a letter isn't mentioned or acknowledged by the recipient, it doesn't mean it hasn't had a powerful impact. Here's an anecdote that proves the point:

Back in 2014 (little more than twenty letters into this hobby), I sent a letter to my wife's BFF from grade school, a wonderful, super-accomplished, and super-attractive woman whose pseud-onym will be Hillary. She was in the throes of divorce—her husband of thirty-odd years had left her for a younger woman. Hillary kept her equanimity, kept her head down, and, as the pri-mary breadwinner in the family, kept earning a living, supporting her daughters in the way she had been doing for years. She never got down into the mud, and there was little of the animosity, bit-terness, and flame-throwing that often accompany these breakups after long-haul marriages, at least not to my knowledge.

So, I sent her a letter expressing admiration, telling her it was a privilege to know her, and that I thought she was a rock. It's now been ten years, and Hillary has never brought up the letter to me. But she did say something to my wife, Elaine, using an expression I've never heard before or since. She said, "Joel's letter took my knees out from under me."

The point being just because it isn't spoken about, isn't mentioned, or never comes up in conversation after the fact does not mean the Letter of Gratitude hasn't had a profound impact on the person who received it.

13

One Dozen Sample Letters

The sample letters in this chapter are meant to be instructive, perhaps even a template, for those considering delving into this highly rewarding hobby. A dozen in total, one example from each calendar year since the first letter was written late in 2013. This sampling, comprising less than 5 percent of the total output, runs the gamut. A few are to family members, and several are to friends—old, new, and resurrected.

Contained herein is something of a "transactional letter," a "fan letter," a group letter, and a letter of condolence/gratitude. Some are more straightforward and serious, others freewheeling. By reviewing the style, which varies from letter to letter, perhaps the reader will gain a few ideas or insights into how they might want to construct letters themselves.

Hopefully this "glance behind the curtain" at my writing style (and the range of recipients) will provide a spark, an idea, or an inspiration as you pursue this hobby yourself.

The **takeaways** of each letter will provide additional pointers regarding what's memorable, unusual, or important to note in each example.

I start with the very first Letter of Gratitude in the archive. Notice that it's so early in the game that the letter is undated! (That happened maybe three or four times from the outset, before I wised up and started dating them.) This letter was written a week or two prior to Thanksgiving **2013**. The recipient is a colleague, mentor, and friend from the golf industry named **Dan Shepherd**. The irony is that when I sat down to write this letter, there was no inkling there would ever be a second letter, never mind hundreds additionally!

Takeaways: When appropriate, reference the recipient's family, even if you don't know them well, or at all. Don't shy away from being direct with both gratitude and praise.

Dear Dan,

I hope this note finds you well, and everything is proceeding smoothly with Cole, Ann, and the home front!

Just wanted to send you a quick note and tell you how grateful I am for your support and friendship over the last dozen or so years. It has truly been a pleasure getting to know you and spend time with you, and my association with you and Buff Comm has been the most fruitful partnership (I suppose with the exception of the Dye Family . . . Halivai!) in my sixteen-plus years writing.

Though we aren't in as close contact these days as we have been in the past, I still think of you often and hope life is continuing to treat you well. While I have met and befriended numerous colleagues and associates in the golf biz since 1998, I can tell you without reservation I consider you my "bestie" in the business, and hope our paths will cross again soon, above/beyond the quick and frenetic "two ships passing in the night" which has been our modus operandi the last few years at the PGA Show in Orlando.

Thanksgiving is looming in a few short weeks, and I sat down to type this note because you are one of the people I feel very thankful to have met and befriended. Golf writing has been good to me in many ways, but right at the top of the heap is the relationships it has allowed me to foster and build, and ours is one I value as much or more than any other I've developed in this business.

Thank you for everything!

Warmly—

This selection from **2014** was written to my uncle **Herb Kandel.** He was gone less than six months after this was sent. It was the first time (but sadly far from the last) when I felt the *tremendous* sense of relief that a letter had been sent to share my feelings and goodwill prior to their passing. The timing of this letter is a picture-book example of a quotation that is part and parcel of every speaking presentation I deliver. Said Ralph Waldo Emerson, "You cannot do a kindness too soon, because you never know how soon it will be too late."

Takeaways: Mentioning something *specific* you're grateful for is always useful.

Don't be afraid to be self-deprecating in a humorous or entertaining manner.

January 18, 2014

Dear Uncle Herb,

Just wanted to write you a quick note and wish you all the best in your recovery. I didn't realize you were battling these different maladies until we all received an "update" email from Cousin Arlene a few weeks ago.

While I wish you a speedy recovery, I will also tell you how much I have appreciated the consistency of the electronic birthday and anniversary cards you have sent me over the years. You are very kind and thoughtful, and in this day and age, when people are moving a mile a minute, taking the time to do that speaks volumes regarding your character.

Truth be told, you have long held a place as my

Favorite Uncle. Granted—the competition hasn't been too stiff—Stanley passed in the '70s or early '80s as I recall, same with Charlie and Sam [my dad's sisters' husbands], and I haven't seen or spoken to Murray since 1965!

However, even had they been in my orbit the last thirty or forty years, I seriously doubt they would have been much competition to you, or have embodied the good-natured humor, the caring, and the cleverness that are all part of your personality. I still remember our visit to you in New Orleans way back in about '72 or so. I recall your Pontiac Trans-Am (?) with the collapsible "nose" on the hood; one of the coolest car features I had ever seen! I recall you taking us to fine dining establishments like Brennan's and Antoine's, and I remember how happy my mom was to be visiting you, spending time with her favorite brother!

Being "Favorite Uncle" is a real honor—I have seven nieces/nephews (other than Al's grown kids) and if I occupy the top spot in any of their minds, I would be absolutely shocked!

Feel better—good thoughts are emanating your way from Savannah!

Dave Stockton, two-time winner of golf's PGA Championship and victorious captain of the 1992 USA Ryder Cup team (generally considered the most memorable, dramatic, and closely contested tournament in that event's nearly century-old history), received a letter in **2015.** The message was predominantly grateful, but slightly transactional, as I was hoping his eminence in the golf world would assist in getting a book sequel off the ground. (Not to be!)

Takeaways: Referencing a date on the calendar (major holiday, start of summer, etc.) can pinpoint a letter and give it context.

Mentioning a mutual friend or acquaintance can provide a conduit and make a letter more meaningful in lieu of a deeper personal relationship.

November 24, 2015

Dear Dave,

I write you this Letter of Gratitude just two days prior to Thanksgiving. There is no better time on the annual calendar to express my thanks to you for being such a tremendous help with this unique book project. I'm not going to say the book wouldn't have happened without you, but I will be quick to admit that your involvement made things far easier, and for that I am extremely grateful.

When I first met Laurie Hammer while writing Pete Dye—Golf Courses *in 2007, I could quickly tell he was cut from a different cloth than most club pros I had encountered previously. He had a warmth and enthusiasm that I found to be rare. When I met his son Kevin subsequently, I was equally impressed. The Hammers helped me get in touch with you—first for some quotes for that book, then you and I spoke at length about the '91 Ryder Cup when I wrote* Kiawah Golf *in 2013, and obviously all our many dealings with the project just completed. So, my thanks to Laurie and Kevin for introducing me to you!*

I hope you enjoy the new book and find it uniquely worthwhile. I imagine you have scores, if not hundreds, of golf books in your personal library but I'm confident in saying there is nothing on your bookshelf quite like this one. I am indebted to my old friend Dave Rafus for giving me the idea, and to you for helping me see it through. You'll notice that I have dedicated the book to the two of you!

Anyway—my best wishes to you and your family this holiday season! As I might have mentioned, I am thinking seriously about writing a sequel to this book. So, if you have additional ideas, or perhaps might be willing to make an introduction to one of your peers who is as charitably oriented as you and might be willing to spearhead the project in the same way you did, I would be most appreciative.

I look forward to hearing your thoughts on the book—thank you again!

In **2016**, I wrote to someone my wife and I originally met in Utah, but who had subsequently returned home to live in Charleston, South Carolina. **Susan Pearlstine** and I hit it off from the get-go, and we would spend time with her in both locales, particularly in the years before we abandoned the Southeast to make our permanent home in the West.

Takeaways: This is a good example of thanking someone for something specific before segueing into a general discussion of gratitude.

Depending on one's relationship with the recipient, don't shy away from referring to their life challenges and ups and downs. It makes the letter more authentic.

June 1, 2016

Dear Susan,

Elaine and I want to thank you for your gracious hospitality in Charleston last week and reiterate what a wonderful time we had at the Old Crow Medicine Show!

However, this is not a mere thank-you note. This is a Letter of Gratitude, and it happens to be the seventy-fifth (!) letter of this kind I've sent since I began this ultra-rewarding hobby back in November 2013. You are well deserving and likely understand the concept of gratitude more than most on my list!

As you know, I am a big fan of yours. You have an ineffable charm, a goodness of spirit, a liveliness, curiosity, and vivacious nature that I find immensely appealing. I am grateful to you not only because you're a consummate hostess with a magnificent new home and an overstocked beer cooler, but because of the generosity of your spirit. Your financial largesse toward MUSC is nothing less than astounding. Your continued support of the arts and culture, your commitment to your magnificent hometown, and the way you immerse yourself in so many arenas simultaneously are examples for everyone to follow.

I also know that despite the "fabulousness" of your life, with the means to be a patron, the wherewithal to travel, etc., you've also endured many difficult times. Between the surgeries, maladies, family dramas, and general whirlwind of life's ups and downs, I've often admired your equanimity and ability to roll with the punches. Not everyone could show the same poise or maintain a similar upbeat disposition.

I would be remiss in not mentioning your garden. It's a blessing you can cultivate such a cornucopia of different plants and vegetables in the corner of your lovely backyard. Likewise, I'm pleased to see your personal garden flourishing so beautifully, with Amy and Dana close at hand, a grandchild coming, and your sister, other family members, and scores of friends on or near the peninsula. Yours is a rich and full life, well deserved. Elaine and I are fortunate to call you a friend.

The letter from **2017** was sent to a young man named **Noah Luskey.** Technically he's the oldest son of some good friends, but over the years, particularly after he left home and went out into the world, we formed a completely independent relationship. I'm pleased to report that some seven years later, in 2024, he and his fiancée received a congratulatory Letter of Gratitude on the eve of their springtime wedding.

Takeaways: Particularly when writing to someone appreciably younger, it's fine to offer (small doses) of advice. But no preaching is necessary.

Letters of Gratitude aren't necessarily cloying like Hallmark cards. There's always room for witticism, a touch of sarcasm, or a bit of snark.

March 10, 2017

Dear Noah,

Just wanted to offer you a quick word of encouragement as you embark upon your exciting new career at Microsoft!

What an exhilarating time in your life—new job, new city, new opportunities to advance both personally and professionally. The next few months, probably the whole of 2017, are going to be a whirlwind! Enjoy it, don't just endure it, because you'll look back on this period in ten or twenty years with nostalgia mixed with pride. Here you are, moving three thousand miles from where you grew up, away from most of the people you know, and beginning what will assuredly be a successful tenure at one of the world's most admired companies. It's all fantastic!

Perhaps you'll be back on the East Coast in a few years. Perhaps you'll never again make a rent or mortgage payment east of the Mississippi. That's what is so cool about your position, as you stand on the precipice of your future. It's all wide open, all possibility, and with your education, natural acumen, and (burgeoning) people skills, your prospects are incredibly bright.

Please know you are always welcome to visit us in Utah; we would be delighted to have you for any long or extra-long weekends, winter or summer. You are an exceptional young man in many ways, and I am grateful to you personally for some (not all) of your guidance as I navigate (and often stumble) through this high-tech world we now live in.

I know your parents and family are swelling with pride, despite the fact that they might get a bit misty-eyed in your cross-continent absence. Don't sweat it—I'll keep them entertained and be happy to kick the dog and the cat (while nobody's looking) and tell them you're thinking of them and miss them as they skitter across the floor!

Mazal tov—your future holds nothing but promise!

While I've written letters addressed to couples on dozens of occasions, there have only been a handful of times where the letter was addressed to a group. In **2018**, I wrote to the **Longmeadow (MA) Class of 1978 40th Reunion Committee** expressing regret after an unexpected health concern scuttled my travel plans and precluded me from attending this milestone event.

Takeaways: Mentioning commonalities (in this case, no less than ten fellow classmates) helps to humanize and provide connection.

If possible, try and conclude a letter with a poignant, memorable, or lyrical turn of phrase.

June 22, 2018

Dear Craig, Betsy, Moira, Maura, et al.,

It pains me to write this Letter of Gratitude prior to the Big Weekend, as I had planned on writing you a note next week or soon thereafter, after the dust had settled.

However, as my late mother often remarked, "Man imposes, God disposes." We all know timing is everything, and in this particular instance, my timing is hideous! I just cannot break away to head east at this time—despite the plane ticket I purchased six weeks ago, the check I sent to Belchertown a month ago, and the haircut (alas—not my bouffant of yesteryear) I commissioned just days ago!

You know I'm not teasing when I tell you I was really looking forward to the Grand Soiree. I eagerly attended and enjoyed myself immensely at our fifth, tenth, twentieth, twenty-fifth, and thirtieth, only missing out on the thirty-fifth, if there even was one. (If so, I didn't hear too much about it.)

I know that this one will top them all, and you have

worked diligently to get the word out to all who allowed themselves to be found. I began a text chain with some of my old pals some months back, attempting, for lack of a better word, a "head count," and many/most of the boys (as well as my oldest friend in the world, Sara, our acquaintance dating from about 1965) will be in attendance. So it's my loss to not slap backs and trade barbs with Finch, Sherman, Dolan, Foley, Boudreaux, Crosby, and Ryno, among others.

Furthermore—and you committee members fall into this category—I was also looking forward to catching up with doz-ens of other classmates with whom I've been friendly but whom I've barely seen or have had little contact with over the years.

Reunions are funny entities. There are likely one hundred of our classmates living in or around town, or within a couple of hours, anyway, who would consider the idea of attending ludicrous. Then—you have (WAY) out-of-towners like Tyler Young and Wendy Wolf (I guess I now fall in the same cate-gory) who make every effort to get there to reminisce, renew old friendships, and catch up. (Perhaps the end-of-the-alphabet syndrome?) There's no rhyme or reason, and the randomness of this decision-making process reminds me of a line we used to use on Wall St: "That's what makes the market."

So—thank you, one and all, for spending your time and energy to put this weekend together. I'm sure it will be (or by the time you get this letter—was) a barn burner. My calculator tells me that at our age, high school has comprised just 7 per-cent of our lives to date, the percentage growing smaller with each passing year. But for some of us, it has a disproportionate hold on who we are, and who we became. I'm wistful as I complete this note, because despite the fact I left Longmeadow more than twenty years ago, Longmeadow never left me.

This letter from **2019** was sent to my Boston-based sister-in-law **Tracy Harris,** married to my wife's brother. We have always had a great rapport and share several synergies. These include a lack of interest in driving a powerboat and irritating our in-laws. If this isn't the most irreverent letter in the archive, it's undoubtedly in the top three.

Takeaways: Letters of Gratitude don't have to be serious or even earnest. They can be silly, cheeky, and humorous.

Touching on commonalities (in this case our shared adventures at the lake) help reinforce a bond.

July 22, 2019

Dear Tracy,

I've zipped around or across Lake Winnipesaukee close to a thousand times over thirty-five years and been an overnight guest on Cow Island on a hundred occasions. Through long experience, I've come to some ironclad conclusions:

- *The Fackowie Shack fridge is the finest repository of malted beverages in Christendom.*

- *The "facilities" behind said Shack—rock-strewn, mossy, pine-needled, private yet open-air—is among the best pissoirs in the Lakes Region.*

- *Al fresco dinner feasts, beef-laden bacchanalias fit for Rasputin, are some of the finest meals I enjoy all year.*

- *You are delightful.*

Your husband is indisputably the Straw That Stirs the Drink. No Emo, no New Hampshire. But you are the bendy straw, the candy-striped flexi straw, the kind that both kids and adults love and covet. (Yes—I know that straws are no longer PC.)

Cynics might conclude that this flowery, obsequious prose is a thoroughly transparent mea culpa, a thinly veiled attempt to make up for decades of verbal, emotional, and psychological abuse I've foisted on you. All the insults, castigations, and aspersions that have come your way for the 4:00 a.m. wake-up calls, the tray scraping, the mind-numbing routine of swimming-biking-running, the purple duct tape decoupage adorning your ancient ski boots, the perverse pleasure you take in consistent fifth place finishes in the matron's division of the local triathlon series. And of course, your status as a canine conveyance clerk. Not (all) true.

Critics might say I'm sucking up to you because your lifetime appointment as bona fide kitchen charwoman allows me the unbridled luxury of never lifting a finger, other than to untie (never tie) the boat or hoist the random garbage bag into the community dumpster. Not (all) true.

The truth: You are a joy to be with. Self-effacing, self-deprecating with a sly wit, even-keeled demeanor, and the unique ability to mangle eight, sometimes nine, of every ten stories you attempt to retell. (Even when I'm sweet, I'm sour.)

In conclusion, remember me as that essential, indispensable apparatus you long for and cannot live without. After the music fades, the conversation wanes, the last lemon is squeezed, and the Tito's is capped. With apologies to Sidney Poitier, In the Heat of the Night, as you kick off the covers when the sultry summer air is trapped in the eaves of our adjoining honeymoon suites, this is what you need to make it till morning (or 4:00 a.m., crazy lady).

The biggest fan you have.

On the occasion of her first birthday, in **2020,** I wrote to my beloved granddaughter **Leslie Meredith.** This letter is distinctive for two reasons: First, it's the *only* letter that's never been sent in the mail (or, in a few select cases, hand-delivered). It was written specifically for inclusion in my 2020 book, *Grateful.* Secondly, it is the single longest letter I've ever written. (These two facts go hand in hand. Every single letter that's been mailed fits concisely on a single, typewritten page. This letter never would've done so.)

Takeaways: Sending a letter at a milestone moment (a birthday, anniversary, major holiday) is uniquely memorable.

Stream of consciousness is an unorthodox but effective method of communication.

November 10, 2020

Dear Leslie,

Today you turn one year old! Happy Birthday, my little beauty, and many happy returns. I've also recently celebrated a milestone birthday, my sixtieth, and you and I have much in common besides being kindred Scorpio spirits. We're both a bit unsteady on our feet, tend to drool, and sleep fitfully. Although at least diapers aren't part of my daily wardrobe. Yet.

It is difficult to express how grateful your grandmother Lainey and I are to have you as part of our lives and family. When your first child has her first child, which becomes the first grandchild, it is a profound and mind-boggling experience. Joyous, certainly, but in the interest of full disclosure, also a bit melancholic. Yet another important milestone, another box checked on the continuum of life.

By the time you can cogitate these words, I hope you will start to fully understand the concept of gratitude. How fortunate you are to be surrounded by so much love. To have parents who are so intelligent, enlightened, articulate, athletic, and empathetic. I only knew one grandparent growing up, and that was for a brief period. Lainey knew two, but one of those was for a brief period. Your mom knew or knows three of her grandparents, and you are lucky to have all four, two of us close at hand, both of us thoroughly invested in your happiness and well-being.

How fortunate you are to have been born in wild, wonderful Utah. You will grow up learning to ski and hike and perhaps mountain bike, probably playing tennis or soccer or softball, amid the amazing grandeur of this magnificent state. Your clan is in perpetual motion. Your grandmother Lainey has spent decades in the health and wellness industry. Your dad is highly coordinated and loves athletics. Your mother, as flexible as Gumby, an elegant skier, makes fitness a priority. Even your mom's grandfather, Papa, your namesake and great-grandfather, still exercises an hour a day, sometimes more, and he is ninety-five years old! Suffice it to say that, while insolence is something your parents will likely deal with in the years to come, indolence is a one-in-a-million proposition.

Only a small percentage of native-born Americans whose parents and grandparents were also born here can speak a second language. How fortunate you are that your polyglot father will teach you Spanish. Not only will you become fluent in two of the world's most popular languages, but you will learn them effortlessly, naturally, as easily as you will learn to walk and feed yourself.

It is amazing to contemplate what the world will be like when you are my age. Not even the most astute futurist can foresee what new evolutions are in the offing. Flying cars? Colonies in space? Legitimate racial and gender equality? Disease eradication? Hypersonic air travel? All I can say is the world we inhabit is a wonderful, terrible, complicated place. There are serious problems both here and abroad. Political instability, poverty, pandemic, social insurrection, climate change, tragedy of every color and stripe. However, there will always be more good in the world than bad. More love than hate and more goodness than evil. Thousands are the wicked, but millions upon millions are the righteous.

Your mom's paternal grandmother, who is my mother, was named Libby. She adored all her grandchildren, none more than your mom and her sister, who of course is your loving aunt Kayla. Libby would often say, "Man imposes, God disposes." This was a fatalistic and complicated way of saying that nothing in life is for certain.

I would be ever grateful to teach you how to throw and catch a Frisbee, catch a ball with either hand, even behind your back! I hope we ski together, maybe someday play some golf, and share books, riddles, jokes, and palindromes. If the fates are fortunate, I will dance at your wedding, but please understand that my days of gravity-suspending Russian splits, which were de rigueur in disco days of yore, and as of this writing, dusted off creakily on only the most auspicious of occasions, will by then be relegated to history's dustbin.

I hope for these, and a hundred other things. But if it's not in the cards, I would be content if you were able to maintain memories of me, even hazy or disjointed ones. Memories that, like my love for you, remain sweet and enduring.

In **2021**, I was absolutely thrilled to hear from an old friend of mine after no less than thirty-five years of zero contact whatsoever. **Karen Massimino** was a woman from my past (sadly, not that kind of past, because she was, and remains, a real beauty!). I couldn't wait to showcase these hard-won letter-writing skills as I thanked her for reappearing in my life.

Takeaways: Even in a stream-of-consciousness-type letter, organization helps. ("My gratitude to you is twofold.")

Referencing luminaries (such as sports heroes) even in a tangential fashion adds some zest. Mentioning commonalities (in this instance, several former co-workers) helps to reinforce bonds from long ago.

March 13, 2021

Dear Karen,

I've stepped to the computer to write letters such as this nearly 190 separate times in the last seven-plus years. I indulge in no other sedentary hobby that provides the same jolt of enjoyment and creativity. Among that voluminous output of warm feelings and sentiment, there are precious few on that long and ever-expanding list of recipients who likely have felt the same sense of pleasure and appreciation that I hope you will feel while reading this communique.

While you are in select company in this regard, there is one area in which you stand alone. There isn't a single soul, alive or deceased, who has received a Letter of Gratitude from me after a "radio silence" of nearly thirty-five years' duration! In this unique and highly personal category, you are a singular sensation—undefeated and untied. You have set a record, like Joe DiMaggio's fifty-six-game hitting streak, like Wilt Chamberlain's hundred-point game, like Tom Brady's seven victories in ten Super Bowl starts, that will never be broken and remain unassailable for all time.

My gratitude to you is twofold. First, I am beyond thrilled you reached out to me on Instagram some weeks ago. It was a delightful shock to hear from you. You see, I generally am the connector, the conduit, the instigator, the fosterer of relationships. I live by Don Corleone's mantra, "Keep your friends close and your enemies closer." From kindergarten to college, Wall Street to Main Street, Lowcountry to Snow Country, ultimate alumni to my decades-long golf writing career, I expend energy to stay in touch and connected with those who've been part of my orbit. Though I've often thought of you, and fondly, I figured you were lost to the sands of time. Therefore, it was a joyful moment when your out-of-the-blue missive reached me. Secondly, our time in each other's company, back in our nascent twenties, fleeting as it was, was great fun. I wasn't a great fit at Ziff-Davis; I knew early on that my tenure would be of short duration. But coming to work, goofing around, and cutting up with you, Mae-Mae, a gal you might recall named Donna Keller-Green, Jim D., trading barbs with a fellow named Rob Ettenson, etc., was consistently enjoyable, and a welcome respite from the drudgery of that job.

Truth be told, I cannot recall even a single escapade,

anecdote, or incident in which we were both involved (other than the photographic evidence of our one-in-a-million meetup in Brussels as my honeymoon was nearing conclusion). But I know we were in each other's company repeatedly and regularly and had a personal connection that was as rare as it was enjoyable.

You'll perhaps recall the silly joke I told you on the phone recently. Two newborns are side by side in the maternity ward. They leave the hospital, live out their lives, and are reunited eighty years later in an assisted living home. Recognizing each other, one says to his counterpart: "So, how was it?"

Though we weren't acquainted as babies, and I'm hopefully still some months away from long-term care, the analogy has legs. We've both been fortunate to have moved on from our Park Avenue cubicles to live interesting, dynamic, fulfilling lives, with enduring romance, family, adventure, and travel as centerpieces. How lucky we've both been—so much to be grateful for!

I hope you'll accept my invitation to visit beautiful Park City. What a pleasure that would be! Because for a brief period, a few short years, long ago and far from here, when we were young(er) and silly(er), you were very special to me. My instincts tell me that, sometime soon, you will fulfill that role again.

There are precious few "fan letters" in my LOG oeuvre, but in **2022**, I reached out to my favorite professional golfer, **Rory McIlroy**. I was composing the letter in my head as he was poised to capture the 150th iteration of the Open Championship (known to most casual fans in the USA as the British Open). Alas, it wasn't to be. So, I made a pivot when stepping to the computer. It was slated to be a congratulatory letter, but I sent it along regardless. While I've had cause to send plenty of gratitude/condolence letters (see 2024's example), this might be the first gratitude/commiseration letter in my archive.

Note for the uninitiated: "The Man from Oz" is Aussie Cameron Smith, who came from far behind on the final day to catch and pass McIlroy. "Zinger" refers to former PGA Tour pro and television commentator Paul Azinger. "Your great friend" refers to Tiger Woods.

Takeaways: Comparing a recipient to other luminaries (or to others who are held in high regard by the writer and/or the recipient) is a nice touch.

If possible, when writing to a public figure, try and use a method that doesn't involve an agent, PR company, management team, and so on. If you have a personal or familial connection that can ensure the recipient receives the letter, that's the ideal outcome.

July 23, 2022

Dear Rory,

By the time you receive this letter, I hope the sting of the Open loss has receded into a dull ache. But as I write it, just a few days after the fact, both you and I, and tens of millions of your ardent fans worldwide, remain acutely disappointed. But what can you do? The Man from Oz wielded thirteen clubs and a magic wand that Sunday afternoon, and as Zinger said of your great friend two decades back, when he was throttling the game, and all who played for a paycheck, "there's no defense in golf."

I was a golf writer for decades, but now I traffic primarily in gratitude. I am grateful you've provided me with such a clear and true rooting interest in the game I love to play and observe. I have found that as I age, fandom wanes a bit as life takes its inevitable twists and turns. My boyhood love of the Red Sox, Patriots, Celtics, and Notre Dame has diminished. These days, I only light up for Steph, Brady, Nadal, and you. All incandescent talents, but Rafa is opaque, and much like the Golden Boy, who inconceivably still remains relevant on the gridiron, both soon to exit stage left.

Truth be told, when I was your age, I felt similarly about Tiger and Phil. But their various imbroglios and missteps have, at least for me, diminished some interest. My sense is that you'll almost certainly avoid these pitfalls and decades from now will have the same eminence that very few achieve. Jack Nicklaus and Tom Watson are among the only golfers coming to mind that, in my opinion, have consistently taken the high road through life.

There've been vats of ink spilled in the press over the years regarding your near-universal appeal. But I think it distills down to you following the simple advice given to you by your dad many years ago, when you were initially making your mark. It's a line I've quoted to others more than once: "You can always be nice, and it won't cost you a penny!"

Speaking of gratitude, I'm certain you're grateful for all you've given golf, and all golf has given you. The Open loss was a gut punch I know, but with your natural ability, work ethic, experience, and "intimidation factor" (maybe not Tiger-esque, but still a real thing), there are many more on-course highlights in your future. I'd be gobsmacked if there's not another Jug (and a jacket!) in your future. After all, you'll be in or close to your prime for at least forty more Majors! It wouldn't surprise me in the least if you pick off as many in the future as you have in the past.

In closing, allow me to wish you all good things as you forge ahead, in golf, and in life. You came on my radar sometime shortly before that Masters misfortune, followed so quickly by the Congressional conquest. I've been astonished and delighted by your various pyrotechnics at Quail Hollow over the years and was on the grounds at Kiawah when you hoisted the heaviest hardware in golf. Keep on doing what you do. I (and plenty of others) will be wishing you well from Park City, Utah!

Molly Blewett is a charter member of our UDC (Unofficial Daughter's Club). This letter from **2023** was written in advance of her wedding. While the majority of my letters contain a certain degree of deep feeling and unvarnished emotion, sometimes when it seems appropriate, when the recipient is someone for whom I have special feelings, I'll add an "extra gear," and be ultra-effusive in sharing my thoughts of gratitude.

Takeaways: It's one thing to tie a letter to an annual holiday. But if you can write on what's hopefully a once-in-a-lifetime day (wedding, graduation, retirement, etc.), it adds an additional layer of importance.

The point of view expressed usually comes exclusively from the letter writer. But if appropriate, it can easily be conveyed from a couple, the family, the office team, and so on.

October 10, 2023

Dear Molly,

It gives me tremendous pleasure to write you this Letter of Gratitude, particularly as it coincides with one of the biggest and most joyous days of your life! I have long anticipated the opportunity to write to you personally, and I'm "grateful" that time is nigh.

You'll likely recall that you were part of a "Chorus Line" letter I wrote to the whole DCC Crew some years ago. (March 31st, 2019, if you're scoring at home.) However, the irony is that while your colleagues from that era, mostly an affable and efficient bunch, have faded into the mists of time, you've come into much sharper focus.

I think you're aware that I've written literally hundreds of these letters. Despite our close-knit and decades-long partnership, Elaine has been referenced within these various communiques very rarely, and often obliquely. This is due mainly to the fact that these letters are deeply personal and meant to convey my feelings exclusively. But you can rest assured that the sentiments following in the ensuing paragraphs come from both of our hearts.

You are an exceptional person, and we adore you. You're industrious, entrepreneurial, equanimous, practical, level-headed, lovable, and sweet. You have a certain je ne sais quoi; an effortless charm that makes you such an endearing individual. We feel fortunate to have spent copious, albeit sporadic, amounts of time in your orbit over the last three or four years.

You've long been one of our favorite people in Park City, and now you stand untouched and unequaled in the smallish burgh of Lyme Regis! (With David a close, though distant, second!) In fact, if ever I'm reinfected with that dreadful, eponymous disease, or every time I wander into that hulking hotel high on the hillside, I will think of you, and fondly.

We celebrated our thirty-seventh anniversary just last month. We wish you a similarly lengthy, adventure-laden union of souls. Make laughter a priority, love each other fiercely, and enjoy the ups, downs, and all-arounds. My goodness, it all goes by so quickly! Wishing you both all the very best. Now, tomorrow, and always.

On more occasions than I wish were necessary, I've written a Letter of Gratitude/Condolence. In **2024**, I wrote to a dear friend of my wife's family named **EJ Foody**, who tragically lost his adult daughter, Tori. Though I don't know EJ or his wife well, I felt compelled to reach out from afar and share our sympathy regarding this devastating loss.

Takeaways: When expressing condolence, be direct and be succinct. No need to overembellish.

Never say to a bereaved individual, "I know how you feel." Even if you've lived through a similar tragedy, no one knows exactly how someone else is feeling. You can, however, offer an appropriate analogy, like the one found toward the end of the fifth paragraph.

January 8, 2024

Dear EJ and Mary Kay,

Though we offered an internet condolence on Caring Bridge, Elaine and I wanted to reach out to offer our sympathy for your devastating loss in a more formal, certainly more comprehensive manner than what we feel would be appropriate in an online forum.

Such a terrible heartbreak, to lose your daughter. Unimaginable. We've been thinking about your family constantly since we heard this awful news a week or so ago. There's not too much an outsider (or for that matter, an insider) can offer, except to say you have our utmost compassion in this trying time. But allow me to offer just a few further thoughts.

Though it will likely be many months from now, and

only when the piercing, ceaseless grief starts to abate, at least intermittently, I hope you can start to be grateful for the many happy times, tender moments, loving interludes, and raucous adventures the two of you, Tori, and Trey all shared together. It's a tough ask at this moment, but eventually you'll be able to focus, at least occasionally, on the wonderful times, the memorable, serious, and silly episodes that are part and parcel of a close-knit family.

Mary Kay, please forgive me but I'm not certain we've ever met. EJ, you and I have been in each other's company on just a few occasions. Perhaps in Marblehead. One time in Park City quite a few years back, not too long ago on Hilton Head, and perhaps once in Tampa? (What can I say, other than life's a blur!)

I know you are an ebullient, fun-loving, adventuresome sort, full of vitality and positive energy. Though I don't know you well, I'm grateful we've crossed paths on the rare occasion. I also know your circle is vast. For a moment, visualize an archery target. The bullseye is your family and closest compadres. I assume Amy (and Lori?) are not far from the center. My in-laws, Pat and Les, who love you like a son, might be a further ring removed. Elaine and I perhaps exist on the outermost ring, but it's more likely that we're on the plywood that braces and supports the target!

My point: There are many, many individuals, just like us, far from your regular orbit, who are sending you positive thoughts and healing energy. The vast majority likely feel somewhat uncomfortable reaching out. But do not mistake their reluctance for indifference. More people than you realize are wishing you and your family well, hoping you can someday mend your broken hearts, and recover, as much as is humanly possible, from this sorrowful turn of events.

As is said among the Jewish people in times of loss, may Tori's memory be a blessing to all who knew and loved her.

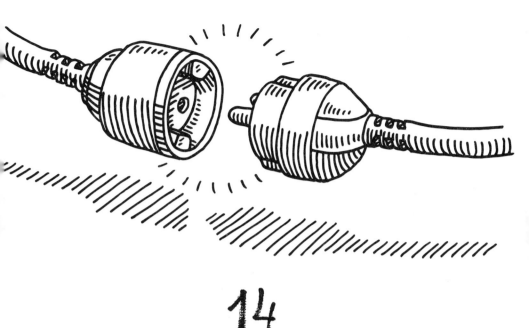

14

Ten Concepts to Jump-Start
Letters of Gratitude

The purpose of this book is to showcase the joys and benefits of writing Letters of Gratitude. However, I harbor no illusions that any reader will embrace this uniquely endearing hobby to the extent I have. Barring unforeseen circumstances, someday I'll eclipse three hundred letters written and sent. That said, my hope is that some readers will enthusiastically write a few dozen, maybe just a dozen, or even a handful of letters. There's benefit in that—even if it turns out to just be a letter or two.

One of the stumbling blocks for potential letter writers is what to say, and how to say it. Here are ten simple concepts that might allow those who don't find expressing themselves easily to develop a framework so they can fully flesh out a letter, beyond a few simple sentences of thanks.

1. Reference the unexpected nature of the letter.

    a. "This letter will come as a shock," "I can only imagine the surprise you are feeling receiving this," and so on.

2. If appropriate, segue from thanking someone for something specific (a gift, favor, invitation, suggestion, etc.) into a general discussion of your gratitude toward that individual.

3. If appropriate, tie the letter to a date, birthday, or anniversary—any milestone on the calendar.

    a. "It's nearly Thanksgiving and a perfect time to offer you my thanks for being part of my life."

    b. "With Christmas around the corner, in this season of good tidings, I wanted to offer you my sincere gratitude for all you've meant to me."

    c. "Next week marks the official start of summer, and I'm so grateful for all those summertime antics we enjoyed together through high school and beyond."

        NOTE: Having written so many letters, I've had cause to stretch this "holiday concept" to the extreme. To wit: In early November 2016, I started a letter to a college pal and teammate named Jimbo thusly: "It's Veteran's Day, and as one of my 'veteran friends,' I wanted to reach out and send you this Letter of Gratitude!"

4. Mention something specific from the past the recipient will certainly remember:

a. "I'm sure you recall my hesitancy to join you and your cousin on that postgraduation trip to the Jersey Shore. Even though it was only a long weekend, it remains one of the fondest memories of my teenage years, and I'm so grateful you convinced me to join in. I think of those youthful escapades as some of the most freeing and exhilarating days of my life."

5. You can show gratitude for something the recipient might not necessarily recall but is burnished in your memory: "I'd be surprised if you recall this brief exchange, but shortly after I came to work at the firm, I was feeling overwhelmed by the workload, and not positive I could pull my weight. Out of the blue you asked me to lunch. When you told me I was doing fine, learning the ropes, and starting to become valuable to the team, my confidence soared. Even now, fifteen years later, I remember your kindness vividly and am so grateful you went out of your way to help the 'new guy on the block.'"

6. Reference the recipient's spouse or family, even if you don't know them personally.

7. Humor is always welcome in a letter. (One exception might be a Letter of Gratitude/Condolence, though done tastefully, it can help momentarily lighten the mood of the bereaved.) A little bit of poking fun, particularly with a closer or longtime friend, adds some zest and memorability to a letter. Here's an actual line I used in a letter: "You are the only person to date who has hit me with a football, tennis ball, Frisbee, and golf ball—the veritable 'Grand Slam' of concussive acts of aggression!"

8. Self-deprecating humor is the safest bet; there's nothing to be taken the wrong way if the writer is poking fun at themselves!

   a. "You're probably surprised to be hearing from me, perhaps because you thought a grocery or 'to-do' list might be the extent of my writing skills."

   b. "I can't tell you how grateful I am for the promotion and the increased responsibility. I never imagined I would make it to the vice presidency in this wonderful organization. Fact is, upon my hiring a decade ago, my brother sarcastically told me he'd be shocked to see me out of the mailroom!"

9. Feel free to mention another individual or individuals in the letter. LOGs are by nature personal thoughts and feelings between the writer and recipient(s). However, there is often cause to speak on behalf of another or others.

   a. "Not only am I personally grateful for that wonderful suggestion regarding our new realtor (doctor, attorney, homebuilder, music teacher, electrician), but my wife, Jane, and our kids are equally pleased and want to pass along their deep gratitude for your assistance."

   b. "My son Alex thrived under your tutelage this past season. Not just he, but many of his teammates as well feel they now have a deeper understanding of the nuance of baseball and its strategy. Even though it's still Little League, because of your patience and enthusiasm, many of your players are grateful they'll have a leg up when it comes to next year's tryouts."

10. If possible and appropriate, end the letter with a heartfelt, poignant, or memorable sentence or two. These three examples have all appeared in letters I've written previously.

A condolence note: "The Hostess City of the South will always hold a special place in our hearts, despite its now diminished charms in Betty's conspicuous absence."

A letter to an old friend: "Though I no longer live in the region, and make my home elsewhere, it is people like you who will always make Longmeadow home."

A letter to a youngish friend, who's life circumstances are in flux: "It pleases me greatly to know that, despite whatever life may have in store for us, and whenever our paths might ultimately diverge, this simple piece of stationery you now hold will always afford us a permanent connection."

15

Be Grateful—Not Gandhi!

Let's begin this chapter with a brief personality quiz:

- How long would you wait directly behind an inattentive or distracted driver once the stoplight turns green, before leaning on your horn (or at least offering a friendly "beep") to get them moving?

- If someone is delaying the elevator door from closing while finishing a conversation with someone *not* entering the elevator, how much time will you allot before clearing your throat or tapping them on the shoulder?

- If the person in the express checkout lane at the grocery store has slightly more than fifteen items or, even worse, pulls out a checkbook, of all archaic items, to pay for their goods, does your blood pressure immediately spike?

- If the person driving ahead of you is matching the speed limit to the decimal or, worse, puttering along two or three miles per hour below the stated limit, do you feel your pulse thundering in your ears in no time flat?

If your answer to any or all these questions is "instantaneously" (or a facsimile thereof), then welcome to my world, and the world of tens upon tens of millions of "Type A" individuals worldwide. (And if you remain mellow and Zen throughout these momentary indignities, taking a few deep breaths, listening to the miracle of your heartbeat, or just scrolling on your phone, I admire you and want to visit the vegan commune where you were raised.)

My point: You can be deeply grateful, proactively grateful, immersed in gratitude, and still have a veritable cornucopia of less-than-ideal personality traits. It's the yin and yang of human existence. Nobody is completely sweetness and light, and nobody is totally demonic and despicable. (Well, there might be a few of the latter, but we're here to talk about gratitude.)

Picture the Scales of Justice. Now reimagine them as the Scales of Human Frailties. For this analogy, picture these embarrassing qualities piled up on the left side of the scale. These negative attributes include, but are not limited to:

- Anger

- Belligerence

- Competitiveness

- Despondency

- Envy

- Fear

- Greed

- Hubris

- Intolerance

- Jealousy

(I could easily go further down the alphabet, perhaps ending with "zombielike," but this chapter is based on a key element of my keynote presentation, and listing ten negative human qualities is more than enough to make my point vividly without enduring pointless brain strain!)

Here's the positive news: If one can add a sizeable dollop of gratitude on the *other side of the scale*, balancing out these negative qualities inherent in every living being, one of two things will happen, both good. If one is truly fortunate, all this deep gratitude will help buff away some of the rough edges of the negative qualities.

However, even if that doesn't happen, and the negative traits remain intact, at least you will also be a grateful person!

Here is a perfect example of this phenomenon. In low moments, I question my efficacy, value, and relevance as a husband, father, grandfather, brother, and friend. I despair about what might be considered my middling skills as a speaker, writer, skier, golfer, mountain biker, and so on. And amid all this negative self-talk, I perk up thinking about one indisputable fact: At least I'm grateful!

Add proactive, expressive gratitude to your life. Do so hour by hour, or at the very least on a daily basis. It will improve your outlook and self-worth, and it will enhance your self-esteem. It's one positive attribute you can *always* have going for you.

16

Grateful When
the World Is Hateful

When I was a stalwart Little Leaguer during the Woodstock era, my first love was baseball. Pure irony, considering decades later my career would meander toward obsessing about, chronicling, and opining about another stick-and-ball pursuit.

While golf has always been a niche sport, baseball has mostly receded from the national zeitgeist. This occurred in the flash it took to go from boyhood to deep middle age. My personal interest in what was once the national pastime has diminished considerably, mirroring national trends. The NFL, NBA, MMA, and even European soccer seem to draw more eyeballs, get more clicks, inspire more conversation, and take up the lion's share of the nation's attention in comparison to the Grand Old Game.

Despite its diminution, baseball expressions still pepper our vernacular. A business success is still a "home run." Rebuffed as a potential suitor? You're said to have "struck out." Life throws everybody curveballs. And most are assaulted with beanballs. It's not a matter of if but when you'll be knocked down. The question becomes, how willing are you to get up, brush off, dig in, and get back in the batter's box?

The problem was, I couldn't get up.

Six weeks ago, writing this, six of us were trekking in the Peruvian Andes, destination Machu Picchu. High on the remote Salkantay Trail, fourteen thousand feet above sea level, all it took was one false step. My right leg slid, my left leg braced, and down I went as if struck by a thunderbolt. There I was, writhing about on the muddy, rocky trail we were descending. As was diagnosed three days later, after an emergency evacuation back to Salt Lake City, it turned out that my left quadriceps tendon had snapped like an overtightened guitar string. But the only revelation conveyed in that moment, after a fruitless attempt to stand up and continue the descent, was that my left leg had been rendered useless in an instant.

Some context: My fiftieth season on skis or a snowboard had concluded just a single day prior to this South American expedition. There had been some (literal) tight spots caused by stupidity and/or hubris, and I'd found myself in scores of untenable positions through the decades, but I never failed to make it off the hill, sometimes a bit worse for wear, under my own power. Similarly, there had been twenty-five years gamboling about with regularity on a mountain bike with no negative effects beyond superficial trauma.

In anticipation of this "bucket list" excursion in Peru, the concern was my heart, lungs, and the altitude. But a lower extremity injury? It never crossed my mind. But from that instantaneous, leg-ruining lightning strike, it's only been off my mind for a few scant minutes at a time.

Though I would typically eschew a guided pony ride around a grassy corral, after the injury, the only option for descent was to be unceremoniously tossed by our guides onto the back of a gargantuan nag, holding on for dear life with two arms and one leg, down a twisting, plunging, rock-strewn crucible.

Sparing the reader additional depressing details, within two hours of returning to the remote lodge where we were domiciled, it was decided an evacuation was necessary. Kind of a no-brainer, considering the next day's itinerary included two thousand feet of gnarly climbing to an altitude above fifteen thousand feet, and I couldn't walk a dozen paces down the carpeted hallway without fear of keeling over.

After packing up quickly, mostly in shock, and urging my wife to continue trekking with our friends, I was ready to depart. Bidding a hasty farewell to the gang, I was transported horizontally from the lodge via mountain stretcher. Six burly Quechuans, all of us wearing what would have been highly ineffectual hardhats should the predicted mudslides develop, carried me some two miles to a shuddering SUV manufactured in the previous century. The vehicle looked as steady and sturdy as its hobbled passenger, but the driver managed to negotiate more than three hours of rutted dirt roads and then dusty byways back to the city of Cuzco. As dusk turned to night on this interminable trip, he deposited me back where this misadventure commenced some five days prior.

Thankfully, the hotel had some ancient crutches in the storeroom, obviating the need for my (now unceremoniously retired) hiking poles. Eighteen hours later, after a long night and an even longer morning and afternoon, escorts arrived for a trip to the airport. Three flights, three semi-inattentive wheelchair attendants, and twenty-three hours later, we landed back in Salt Lake City—nearly a full week earlier than what had been planned.

Grateful when the world is hateful—to me, it means attempting to see the glass as half full, which isn't easy in dire circumstances. I'll use G and H to alternately designate the mixed torrent of emotions and internal turmoil as this calamity played out and continues to impact me in this moment.

H—The trip was ruined, well in advance of the ultimate destination.

G—My wife and our friends, despite whatever pall was cast in my absence, made it to journey's end.

H—The forty-eight hours it took from accident, evacuation, separation, and isolation to the home airport, I wouldn't wish on anybody. I still have a low-level version of PTSD. The title of an underrated Mel Brooks film from 1977 sums it up best: *High Anxiety*.

G—I saw my daughters, grandkids, and crackerjack orthopedic doctors within a few days of my unexpected return.

H—The week spent at home alone, crutching around presurgery, was a toxic brew of FOMO, jealousy, and despair, while my wife and crew soldiered on amid the beauty and grandeur of the lush, mountainous Peruvian landscape.

G—The surgery was performed by the preferred orthopod just eight days post-accident. Really remarkable considering where the injury occurred, the circuitous journey home, and the unrelenting patient schedule that these doctors are burdened with due to the seemingly never-abating supply of battered citizenry.

H—I'm mostly stuck on the couch or the porch, communing with an insidious leg brace, either bound to my limb or within arm's reach 24/7.

G—Because it's my left leg that's currently compromised, driving is possible. Furthermore, I can move about, albeit lopsidedly, on crutches, or in peg-leg fashion. Furthermore, there's been little pain involved from the outset—just severe immobility.

H—A large swath of this summer will be devoted to rehab. My usual pastimes aren't on the near-term or even mid-term horizon.

G—As opposed to bingeing *Judge Judy* or *Dr. Phil*, or melting my brain with marathon sessions of *Candy Crush* or *Fortnite* (just kidding—never touched either!), there is an inordinate amount of time to work on *Gratitude Tiger*. The book was outlined in rough form in the weeks prior to this ill-fated excursion and was supposed to be written piecemeal throughout the summer months and into autumn. But due to these sedentary circumstances, it's progressing at an accelerated pace. I'm fortunate to have this project squarely on my plate during this extended downtime.

All that said, there's no symphony forthcoming from a micro-Stradivarius. In the big picture, this is something that will pass. In the duration of a lifetime, it's hopefully just an annoying, dispiriting, sleep-diminishing, unexpected speed bump. There are *hundreds of millions*, truly billions of people suffering circumstances far worse than being a slave to a leg brace and a boring summer with minimal outdoor activity. In the overall scheme of things, these worries are nothing but tinsel on the Trouble Tree. Things could be exponentially worse.

Here are six individuals in my orbit who wouldn't wait a

heartbeat to trade their current circumstances for my own. They are friends and friendly acquaintances from the here and now, from the past, and from long ago. All of them are hurting. Yet they deal with their afflictions and low-down, rotten luck with an incredible degree of grace and gratitude.

(Brief aside: They have all received Letters of Gratitude. I've reached out because they inspire with their steadfastness in the face of hardships, and they illuminate a path out of the darkness. I wrote to them because the purpose of these letters is to provide a lift, a moment of pleasure, or at the very least a distraction from the sobering reality of their situations.)

Brad Kaufman and I have been acquainted for about five years. He's affable, athletic, and fun to be around. He's been a highly successful attorney and the co-president at a legal behemoth with offices around the globe and three thousand lawyers on the payroll.

"I come from a long line of men who died in their forties and fifties. I only know of one who made it into his sixties," begins the New York–born Kaufman, who moved to Florida as a toddler.

"I was convinced it wasn't bad genes, just bad lifestyles. As a result, I committed myself to being fit. Playing league sports into my fifties, an avid runner, skier, mountain and road biker, and a gym rat. At fifty-four, I completed the 2014 Boston Marathon. Unfortunately, I developed 'runner's knee' syndrome, so my running life abruptly ended in 2015. But there were many activities I still enjoyed.

"I turned sixty in 2020, breaking the age barrier that so many men in my family failed to reach! I felt vindicated—it *was* lifestyle, not genes, that had been the culprit after all."

Kaufman hesitated for a moment, then continued. "My celebration was short-lived. Within a year or so after this milestone birthday, my health went into rapid decline. I was having difficulty seeing straight and went from climbing mountains to being out of breath just climbing the stairs in my home. My ancestors were surely laughing now. All that time I spent in the gym, running, et cetera, I could have been boozing it up, eating what I felt like, and smoking cigars!"

Kaufman developed multiple health challenges nearly simultaneously. "I was diagnosed with suspected gliomas in the frontal lobes of my brain, my left eye became badly misaligned and required surgery, I was diagnosed with two related autoimmune diseases and finally blood cancer. Specifically, myeloma. I have been in treatment for myeloma since the summer of 2023."

The father of three went from being constantly in motion to constantly in hospitals or wearing out his favorite pillows on the couch. "While I put on a happy, positive outlook, in reality I was dealing with a growing depression caused not only by the loss of the quality of my life but also by the impact my illness was having on my wife of thirty-six years and our adult children," admits Kaufman.

"I was feeling like a burden and like I was no longer capable of contributing anything of value. But many things have helped me deal with these sudden catastrophic changes. First, the incredible support from my wife, Jill. You can't imagine how many hours she has spent in multiple hospitals around the country, asking all the right questions and keeping me up for the fight.

"My brother and sister have both been there every step of the way. My friends and my law firm have been unbelievable as well. Our young attorneys from around the globe made a very special film offering their support and encouragement, for which I was very grateful. I felt like Jimmy Stewart's character in *It's a Wonderful Life*. But for my illness I would never have seen that I had touched so many people and made some small difference in their lives.

"Nevertheless, I was still struggling with finding a purpose for my current very inactive life. That changed starting on October 7, 2023," states Kaufman, referencing his renewed sense of determination. "Hamas attacked Israel and killed more than twelve hundred people and kidnapped hundreds more. Since then, I have been actively engaged in advising and representing victims of this unprovoked attack, students suffering antisemitism on campus, and involved with an organization calling out antisemitic behavior.

"This has given me a purpose, and I am grateful for the opportunity to serve my community. So, what have I learned from this journey? Run a little less; drink a little more; spend less time with people who don't get you and more time with people who do. And don't forgo that fatty food! After all, it really is the best!" So concludes Brad Kaufman, who fights hard for those suffering in Israel while fighting hard for himself.

Ron Jackenthal lost his son Sam to a freakish skiing accident in 2015. We became acquainted some years later, right about the time he started the Live Like Sam Foundation in his son's memory. During the last several years, Ron and I have begun skiing together occasionally and generally spending more time in each other's company.

"Even though he was just sixteen at the time, Sam was the men's 18 and under overall US Junior National Freestyle Ski Champion. He was training with his team in Australia and suffered a catastrophic injury. After a monthlong hospital stay, Sam finally succumbed." So begins this tragic but hopeful story, as told by his loving father.

"Our town, Park City, Utah, has a full-time population of eight thousand. But returning home after Sam's passing, more than fourteen hundred people showed up for a celebration of life for my son, a sixteen-year-old boy," continues Ron, still with a sense of wonder nearly a decade later. "What made Sam so special wasn't his athletic accomplishment but the way he showed up in the world for himself and others. Sam was an incredibly positive, kind, generous, fun, and empathetic human. He was a passionate, driven young man who lived each day as if it were his last.

"As a grieving parent, I've realized there are two silos of grief for a parent who has lost a child, regardless of their child's age. The first silo is the loss of a child. I believe this is a similar experience for most grieving parents, no matter the child's age. We all experience trauma and loss that no one should ever go through. The second silo is the silo of circumstance. Parents who lose a child to overdose or suicide (I am purposely skipping something unimaginable like murder) have a very different and often haunting experience compared to parents who've lost a child to an accident or a life-ending health issue. This is because most parents who lose their children to overdose or suicide are haunted by guilt and the ever-present thoughts of what they could've done differently; perhaps they could have gotten their child more resources or given them tough love and ultimately saved their life."

Ron used to be in tech sales, but he ultimately changed his focus. "It became clear to my daughter Skylar, who is two years younger than her brother (just fourteen then and now in her early twenties), and me that we needed to create a youth-focused foundation honoring Sam's legacy. The tricky part was that it wasn't clear what the foundation would stand for and how we would help. After all, Sam was a mentally and emotionally healthy teenage boy. For example, mothers against drunk driving makes logical sense. Fathers against healthy and high-functioning national sports champions, not so much!

"It wasn't until I went on my own personal trauma recovery and grief journey, four years after Sam's passing, that I was able to connect the dots between Sam's life and impacting our youth today. Through recovery work with professionals and other parents, I started to see a pattern emerge. It became clear to me that 80 percent of our youth that we're losing were dying from overdose or suicide. With the guidance from leading educators and mental health experts (plus guidance from Sam), Skylar and I created the Live Like Sam Foundation.

"Now in our fifth year, we are the premier youth, well-being, and prevention nonprofit in our area. We provide numerous youth well-being programs, including our evidence-based program called Thrive, impacting thousands of young people. Our foundation's goal is to create a community of resilient youth with a healthy sense of self. It is proven that with heathy self-esteem and resiliency, we can handle many of our challenges. I am grateful every day that we were able to create this nonprofit and make positive changes in our community.

"There are still incredibly painful and lonely days," concludes Ron, a New Yorker by birth who's been in Utah some twenty-five years. "While Sam is no longer physically here, his presence continues to surround us all and inspire us to live a better life. We are encouraged to celebrate Sam's life and legacy every day. Thousands of young people, their families, teachers, and health professionals all know the importance and benefits of 'Living Like Sam.' It's clear that my son's legacy will continue to soar and positively impact generations to come. We also know Sam wants all of us to live in the moment, dream big, and laugh often."

Pam Grayboff and I rode the summer camp bus together when we were eight or nine years old. Eventually we graduated high school together. But it's accurate to say we've been in communication (predominantly through text and email) far more in the last five years than we were in the first fifty. Pam is now in her sixth year of battling ALS. Her resilient spirit is awe-inspiring.

"When I was first diagnosed with ALS in 2018 at the age of fifty-eight, I had no idea how drastically my life would change. I used to rush through life trying to get to the next thing, accomplishing my goals and bucket list. I am glad I did; look at me now." So begins this hometown girl of mine, sharing her sorrowful but uplifting journey.

"I really learned a new dimension of having patience when I quickly became a quadriplegic from ALS. I can't do anything for myself; I'm trapped inside my body from my shoulders to my toes. When life happened, I had no choice but to find patience and joy in being still. I rediscovered the meaning of gratitude and love around me and in my life beyond the unconditional love of my family. My caregivers help me out of the goodness of their hearts as we power through these difficult days together. This has been a lesson in itself."

Athletic and enthusiastic, Pam was a standout tennis player in college and stayed extremely active through adulthood. "I am losing my voice," she says. "It's quite hoarse and weak, so not too much time is spent on the phone anymore. Yet I don't miss out on my daily call to my ninety-five-year-old mom, who can catch maybe half of what I can say. It's been quite frustrating not being able to be clearly heard or understood."

Always optimistic, Pam sees what most would find as an insurmountable obstacle as just another hurdle that needs clearing.

"The good news is my new communication device arrived recently, and I'll get it up and running. Several years ago, I anticipated this could happen. Fortunately, I was awarded a grant from Steve Gleason's foundation in collaboration with Beth Israel Hospital speech pathologists," explains Pam, referring to the former NFL player who is also battling ALS. "I preserved my voice when it was strong with the help of Google AI technology. I will be relying on a synthesized voice with my super high-tech tablet that features eye gaze interaction. So, through this Windows-based device, I will be doing everything I can by operating exclusively through my eyes. It's a huge learning curve and just another challenge I need to overcome. But I'm technically oriented, so I will get this absorbed and figure it out. In fact, I'm writing this email using eye gaze technology!"

Pam was a travel industry executive and in-demand hotel consultant, and she had seen and done plenty on the world stage prior to her illness. "I take pleasure by reclining in my high-tech power wheelchair outdoors and listening to the birds more clearly than I ever did previously. It's a different sense of happiness for life's simple pleasures. I feel grateful to be alive, and in its own way, it compares to hiking and experiencing the extraordinary beauty of New Zealand and the Canadian Rockies, to name just a couple of locations I was fortunate to visit."

Pam maintains an unusually upbeat demeanor despite the mounting and compounding problems of life. "In mid-2023, I started developing serious swallowing difficulties. By January of 2024, I started on pureed meals. Several months later, I had a PEG tube inserted for medications and feeding. I try not to dwell on my former life and career perks, such as when I was dining elaborately in the Caribbean, or throughout Europe, or in Oceania.

However, I still enjoy sipping my morning coffee, drinking my smoothie, and I won't be giving up eating ice cream! The truth is it was a big transition, and I struggled for months to implement this new routine. Glad to say that things are settled down and I am now stable."

Stable describes her mindset. Perhaps even serene? "I wish I was closer to family," states the longtime Atlanta resident ruefully. "But the complexity of this illness makes travel impossible. I wish I could still stroll the beach at sunset, as I often did wherever in the world my travels took me. But I am hanging in there and certainly feel I am one of the lucky ones to still be here, within the small percentage of ALS sufferers still surviving five years past diagnosis. I have no plans to leave this earth anytime soon," continues this astounding woman, a living example of bravery in the face of adversity.

"I'm grateful because I have experienced surprises of overwhelming support and random acts of kindness and generosity from friends, neighbors, acquaintances, and even strangers during this challenging journey. It has taught me the true meaning of human kindness and the importance of deep appreciation. I focus on finding happiness in the present moment and in just being. I am an optimist, and every day I must recommit myself to keep fighting onward," concludes the Unsinkable Pam Grayboff, a one-of-a-kind fighter who has managed to find peace within utter stillness while remaining dynamic in her mind and heart.

Heather and Rob Mansson are a couple I've met in person on just a few occasions. Fate and its capricious nature threw us together just a few months ago as I write these words. They endured the heartache of losing their youngest daughter, Parker, who suffered from soft-tissue sarcoma, in spring 2022. "Little P," as she was known, was just eleven years old.

"We moved to Utah from Charlotte, North Carolina, during the pandemic," begins Heather. "Something seemed off with Parker just as we were arriving, and I brought her to the pediatrician that very day." Within a month of that seemingly innocuous doctor's visit, Parker was admitted to Primary Children's Hospital in Salt Lake City for the first time. During her illness, which was nearly two years in duration, she spent upward of one hundred days hospitalized.

"Finding gratitude," says Rob with a sigh, "that's the tricky part. There are certainly moments that are sprinkled in amid the difficult times. The people that came out of the woodwork to support us while Parker was sick and then after she passed. Reminiscing now, after the fact, as we discuss our family's journey. But these are just brief moments."

Rob describes these intermittent moments as specks of light amid a dark journey. "There are glimmers, moments of hope, that alleviate the crushing fear and dread. You reach your breaking point, sometimes going beyond your breaking point. Then it could be a good scan, an unexpected conversation with a caregiver or doctor . . . you never know where it might come from."

Heather, a yoga instructor and mother to teenagers Maisey and Gates, attempts to shed light on the inexplicable. "We were in such a survival mode during her illness I wouldn't say I ever truly felt gratitude. It was blocked. There were moments of hope if we received some good news, which was rare. Whatever gratitude there has been came later, after she was gone, as we were able to look back. That's when the light would come through."

Within a month or so of Parker's passing, the Manssons created a nonprofit called the Little P Project, in her honor, which raises funds for sarcoma research. They've been remarkably successful, considering that when they came to Utah, they had very few friends or contacts. "As I reminisce, I'm grateful we moved to this beautiful place where Parker and her siblings made friends quickly, where she was able to heal and recover, and connect back to nature. I'm grateful for her wonderful care team, Dr. Douglas Fair in particular, with whom we'll always remain close. He and Parker had a special bond, and I don't know if we'd have had someone like that if we had remained in North Carolina."

Both Heather and Rob were amazed at how the community rallied behind them in their darkest time. "Nobody turned away from us—we were welcomed and supported even though we were newcomers and barely knew anyone in the area," continues Heather. She admits they dealt with what she refers to as a "vanishing component" from people already in their orbit. "Some individuals cannot handle the pain or grief and choose not to engage. It's part of human nature. It's hurtful. But it also serves to amplify the individuals who are there, creating meaningful bonds that were unexpected."

As a yogi, Heather attempted to keep up with her long-standing gratitude practice during Parker's illness. But it felt off-kilter and false. "I was going through the motions. When your baby is so sick, it's hard to be grateful for a sunny day, or a delicious dessert, or a stranger's smile."

"We were relying on hope, even just a toehold, to turn the ship around," recalls Rob, who works in finance. "This might sound odd, but I'm grateful we remained hopeful during Parker's illness. To do otherwise, to be overwhelmed by the crushing fear, would have made it all that much worse. When I think about Parker, her life, her spirit, and what she embodied, I feel grateful for that. She was funny, full of life and energy. One of her nurses summed it up when she remarked, 'That little girl is cute as a button and tough as nails.'

"I'm glad the nonprofit raises funds for science and helps families in need," continues Rob. "But beyond that, I'm more grateful that people who didn't know her get to meet Parker through our gala. It carries her message of joy, humor, and zest for life. She represents so many of the traits parents want for their kids and many kids hope to have for themselves.

"The grateful mindset takes work," concludes Rob Mansson. "It's easy to slip back into depression, anger, and frustration. But I try to think of Parker—how she was and would want us to be: living in the moment, finding joy and wonderment in all circumstances."

This family of five also had to learn to live as a family of four, which wasn't easy at first. "I would have preferred to have never started this nonprofit, modestly successful as it's been. It's nice that we've created meaning and a legacy and raised much-needed funds for vital research into this disease," concludes Heather. "I'm proud of our kids, and how they've chosen to live their lives since their younger sister's passing and keep her legacy alive. I am immensely grateful I'm Parker Mansson's mom, and while I wish we'd had her for a lifetime, I'm grateful we had her for eleven incredible years."

Israel Schepps and I are from the same region in western Massachusetts. He is a golf-and-travel buddy from some thirty-five years ago. I couldn't guess the last time we were face-to-face, but it's got to be closer to twenty years than fifteen. Since we last teed it up, had a laugh, or drank a beer, Izzy's been slammed with a cascading series of calamities. Unlike the individuals preceding him in this chapter, all of whom can point to a *singular* devastating incident when their lives took a tragic turn, Schepps has been pummeled repeatedly over the last fifteen years. Yet he retains his sly sense of humor, and, despite these recurring body blows, stays as positive as possible.

"I'm now in the latter half of my sixties, and through this long life I have experienced significant events that have brought me great joy and others that have been ginormous, painful challenges," begins Schepps. "I have always tried to appreciate special times and live in the moment. For example, I know I have cherished my golf-and-travel experiences with my buddies and do not take these events for granted. Many people without the types of trouble and heartache I've endured take these events as entitlements, but not me!

"I have had the joy of a wonderful marriage to my wife, Chris, and our three children, Hillary, Liza, and Max, all of whom have excelled. I could not be a prouder parent. I'm blessed with two wonderful grandchildren. The good news is I see and interact with them regularly via FaceTime. The bad news is they live in Italy with my daughter Hillary, who moved overseas after graduating from Yale some fifteen years ago and has settled there with her Italian husband!"

The first wave of trouble came in the workplace. "My family business failed in 2009 due to the collapse of the American automobile industry in 2008. My textile company was forced to reinvent itself multiple times and in 2000 did so again. We became certified as one of only five entities that produced airbags for the American automobile industry, adhering to the strict rules of the International Standards Organization and customer-specific requirements. Unfortunately, during this 'too big to fail' period of 2007–2009, we were not able to survive," he explains wistfully. "The United States had been manufacturing sixteen million new cars annually, but that dwindled down to seven million. The government bailed out the top companies like Ford and General Motors, but they let the entire automobile supply chain go out of business. This was life-altering for the millions of individuals and thousands of businesses 'downstream' from the Big Three."

The banks called the loans on most businesses and held them accountable for events totally beyond their control. "Our bank called in their loans, and I was held liable for my company's debts even though these debts were caused by our customers and suppliers from the auto industry. A travesty of justice ensued, with a lifetime of personal indebtedness and dispiriting, yearslong legal entanglements that had a profound effect on my family and me personally.

"I was put in a situation where I either could feel sorry for myself or move forward," continues Schepps. "I decided to embrace change, beginning a new job shortly thereafter as a salesman in the commercial roofing industry, where I underwent a crash course in how to outsmart the rain—this after nearly thirty years in the only job I had known since college.

"My former company had been a major employer in the city of Holyoke, Massachusetts, and I was involved in the leadership of the local Chamber of Commerce and Rotary Club. I optimistically thought the demand for automobile airbags would be a lifetime niche for my former company, but it didn't turn out that way. The bank forced me to step down amid this turmoil, causing me to pay a steep price in more ways than one. Personally, professionally, my family and my finances all suffered greatly."

More heartache took the form of knee ache. After decades of dedicated running and road racing, Israel's knees deteriorated to the point where the sport became untenable. "Running was such a stress-reliever amid all the angst and turmoil that had enveloped me," he says.

Out of necessity, Israel's wife, Chris, reentered the work world after many years spent raising their children. "Chris found success as a real estate agent. She was a people person who went on to help her clients buy and sell many houses and made a multitude of new 'besties' in the process. Like me, my wife was very resilient. We persevered and forged forward despite our financial challenges and changes in lifestyle."

The gut punch that followed was arguably the worst of them all. "My family and I were blindsided with another devastating loss when Chris died suddenly and unexpectedly in December 2020," said Schepps, sighing. "My best friend and partner gone, literally overnight, at the age of sixty-three. And to top it off, autopsies were unavailable during the pandemic. My children and I were left with no answers and large holes in our hearts."

Not even two years later, another life-altering tragedy occurred when Israel's sister, Sara, his only sibling and lifetime confidant, died from a glioblastoma brain tumor. "*Poof*, the two people closest to me in life were no longer there. I was shell-shocked but had to move on again."

Then his own health issues took center stage. "In a five-year period, I underwent four significant surgeries. This is despite a lifetime of daily exercise and dedicated fitness routines. I had two knees replaced and then a hip replacement. Joints wear out, and I suppose my decades-long devotion to staying in shape took its toll. But totally unexpected was major heart surgery requiring a triple bypass and other issues. I had a nearly nine-hour procedure and went through intense rehabilitation to regain my health. Some golfers joke that they would rather have a double bypass than a triple bogey. Don't believe it! One of my coping mechanisms is to utilize humor whenever possible. Occasionally I think aloud and might make an inappropriate comment or a bad 'dad joke,' but it's what I do in order to cope with the hand I've been dealt.

"My strategy is focused on short-term appreciation. I try to enjoy milestones and celebrations with my family and friends and savor the moments while they're happening. I try to have the mental fortitude to not feel sorry for myself and my children and to take nothing for granted. I live each day looking for as many positives as possible and not dwelling on past tragedies that can't be undone. It isn't easy to go through life channeling only positive emotions, but that has been my goal.

"These experiences with horrible circumstances, over and over, have not made me feel gratitude. But they have forced me to be resilient, and I have risen to the occasion." So concludes my old pal Israel, a man whose company I enjoyed in person on one hundred happy occasions when we were younger, stronger, and looking forward to what the world might offer us—and before life began taking its toll.

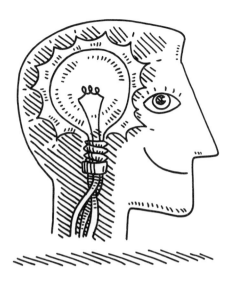

17

Flexing Your Gratitude Muscle

Learning to be consistently, proactively grateful is a skill that needs to be honed. It's no different than learning a foreign language, gaining proficiency in playing the piano, or becoming adept at juggling. It takes dedicated practice.

However, it's easier than these stated examples. Some people have no ear for language or music. And juggling requires a certain degree of dexterity that not all individuals possess. But everyone has the capacity to feel gratitude!

The following exercises will assist in sharpening that focus, provide a grateful mindset, and allow proactive gratitude to flow more freely. Think of it this way: Everyone has a "gratitude spigot." The unfortunate among us, those who have a harder time showing positive emotions or usually see the glass as half empty, possess a spigot that is nearly shut tight. It's rusty from lack of use, allowing for just the occasional drip. Many other spigots allow for a trickle, while others emit a steady stream. It's only the fortunate among us who can "gush" gratitude to any, many, and all. But in considering some of these questions and opening one's mind to the possibility of deeper gratitude, all will be able to loosen the spigot, even just a bit, and allow that life-affirming gratitude to flow more easily.

1. *Think of two individuals for whom you feel gratitude*—one that's still with you, the other, sadly, no longer with you. For all but the most isolated individuals, those who've suffered through life with barely a modicum of support, this is an easy question. It should be practically a reflex answer.

>So, let's raise the stakes: Answer the question for a second time. Think of two more individuals for whom you feel gratitude—one with you, one no longer with you.
>
>Now take it up one notch further. Answer the question for a third and final time. Most readers should hopefully be able to identify at least three people in their life for whom they feel gratitude and reminisce fondly about three others who are no longer with them.

2. *Think of two individuals for whom you feel gratitude*—one that you're grateful to *in general*, and the other you're grateful to for *one specific reason*. Examples of the latter might include:

- A coach who urged you to develop a specialized skill to make the varsity team

- A camp counselor who instilled confidence

- A friend, classmate, or co-worker who suggested you take up a hobby that ultimately became a passion

- A guidance counselor who suggested a certain college or major

- A boss who became a mentor

- A neighbor who offered a summer job that became a vocation

- A stranger who offered a kind word or gesture during a low moment

- A policeman or law enforcement officer who "let something go" when they could've escalated the situation

- An EMT or medical professional who assisted in a time of crisis

- A teacher who inspired your imagination to pursue a field of study

- An advisor or consultant who steered you to an investment or course of action that ultimately bore fruit

From a personal standpoint, I have a "reflex response" to the second part of Question #2 that will mirror many individuals' quick response to Question #1. In other words, someone immediately comes to mind.

When thinking of a person I'm grateful to for a specific reason, Kyle Poplin comes to mind. He was the editor of the *Carolina Morning News* on Hilton Head Island, South Carolina, through much of the

1990s and for several years after the turn of this century.

In the autumn of 1997, for no discernible reason, he hired me to be the paper's golf columnist. (He always claimed that nobody else applied, but that's hard to fathom, and I've never pressed him to find out if he was kidding!)

That columnist position jump-started this author's writing career and was the catalyst for all that has occurred, writing- and speaking-wise subsequently. I like Kyle personally, though we haven't crossed paths in ages, and I am grateful to him in general. (In fact, three or four of my early books were dedicated to him!) However, when thinking of someone I'm grateful to for one single reason, it's "Pop" hands down! (Needless to say, he received a Letter of Gratitude in late November of 2014, just over a year after beginning what has evolved into this lifelong letter-writing endeavor.)

3. *Think of someone for whom you feel gratitude*, not because of what they've done for *you* or how they've enhanced or improved your own life, but for something they've done for *someone else*. Examples might include:

- A doctor or surgeon who saved the life of a loved one or close friend

- A legal or accounting professional who helped extricate a family member or dear friend from bankruptcy or financial calamity

- A firefighter or first responder whose decisive action and expertise saved the day (and perhaps a life) in an emergency

- A life coach, psychologist, or psychiatrist who helped extricate someone close to you from a dark place

- An in-law (or in-laws) who raised their child to be an upstanding, ethical citizen and ultimately a loving spouse, resulting in a happy union with your own child

4. *Think of an individual (or individuals) for whom you're grateful for what they've done for you and for others.* Examples might include:

- A medical pioneer like Jonas Salk, who alleviated the suffering of millions afflicted with polio

- A musical artist or group that uplifts and inspires the imagination, whose live performances are a revelatory experience, who seems to be speaking directly to you in their song lyrics—someone like Bruce Springsteen (or Taylor Swift, 50 Cent, the Rolling Stones, or U2)

- A sports hero like Tom Brady (or Derek Jeter, Caitlin Clark, Lionel Messi, or Simone Biles) whose dedication, focus, and talent led their team to multiple championships, earning the affection and admiration of generations of fans

- Someone who founded a charitable endeavor that resonates, such as Frank Siller, who created the Tunnels to Towers charity after the death of his younger brother Stephen, a firefighter who died on 9/11, or Candice Lightner, who, after the tragic hit-and-run death of her teenage daughter, founded MADD (Mothers Against Drunk Driving)

- A religious or spiritual leader who provides a guiding light or inspiration—a local clergyperson such as a rabbi, priest, pastor, or imam. Or an international figure such as the pope or the Dalai Lama.

- A political figure or government authority who has enacted and passed meaningful legislation to benefit large segments of the population

5. This final question is a simple but revealing exercise to showcase how gratitude should be in the forefront of our minds more consistently. But most people prioritize other things that aren't nearly as important or impactful.

Can you name, off the top of your head:

- The last three teams to win the Super Bowl?

- The last three NCAA football champs?

- The last three Masters champions?

- The last three men's or women's winners of Wimbledon?

- The last three NBA champions?

- The last three vice presidents?

- The last three governors of your state?

- The last three Best Picture winners?

- The last three Best Actor/Best Actress winners?

- The last three movies, plays, or concerts you attended?

The answer is "highly unlikely," to any, many, or all of those questions. But anyone and everyone should be able to list at least three people for whom they feel grateful!

18

GRATITUDE—the Acronym

This will be the third and last acronym found within these pages. (A little goes a long way!) The first was provided by Olympic champion Picabo Street in the Foreword. She used a TIGER acronym to describe her life philosophy. And chapter three uses the same acronym in a completely different context to illustrate that embracing deep gratitude can enhance your life in myriad ways.

This chapter's acronym is a summation of how this letter-writing life almost seems preordained and expresses a philosophy that predates my first official Letter of Gratitude by many decades.

Growing up among writers, published or otherwise, shaped my outlook.

Reaching out, in longhand, on stationery, was de rigueur.

Admittedly, this style of communication is now considered passe.

Taking the time to write, stamp, and mail seems like the relic of a bygone era.

Instagram, TikTok, X, and all other forms of social media have their place.

Though there is something more permanent, almost ceremonial, about receiving a letter by mail.

Unusual, yes. But completely out of fashion? Not now, or ever.

Deciding to share thoughts and feelings in this manner requires more effort.

Enriching is an ideal word to describe this wonderful hobby, which has taken on a life of its own.

19

Wrapping Up This Text with a Brief Word About Texts

As this is the last comprehensive chapter in the book, let me share a brief anecdote about my late father, Karl Zuckerman. Parenthetically, he was an inveterate letter writer himself, which obviously was a trait that passed to the succeeding generation. The difference is he wrote in a mostly decipherable longhand, which of course did not allow him to archive and collate letters in the same obsessive manner as I have. Furthermore, his subjects were varied; he wasn't singularly focused. Instead, he shared deep thoughts on a range of subjects, including education, future promise, the state of the world, the vagaries and complexities of life, navigating personal relationships, and achieving one's potential. This is a stark contrast to me, nothing but a one-trick pony.

Despite our shared bloodline and compulsion to share thoughts via the written word, we had vastly different origin stories. I grew up with a bicycle, a baseball glove, birthday cake, and bowling parties. As a parentless boy, my dad fought to stay alive and protect the lives of his younger sisters.

He died in 1991, when I was thirty years old. He was fifty-four upon my birth as the last of his four children, and by the time I was ready to cogitate any advice, or take to heart any words of wisdom, the teenage years had begun, and he was nearing seventy.

He was a wise and worldly man. As a child, he had lived through the hellish outbreak of World War I in a mud-strewn shtetl in what eventually became Russia. He emigrated to America and over the course of a lifetime built a business and family, and in so doing he became a well-known and respected member of his community. In short, he had basically seen it all.

He offered several sage pieces of advice during my mercurial teenage years before he sadly began a physical and cognitive decline. One that always resonated was this: "If someone asks you for a favor, and it's not a backbreaking request (he was probably referring to an 5:00 a.m. airport drop-off or helping pack up someone's entire household over a long weekend), you should always do your best to assist."

This simple philosophy has been a guiding force for me during these intense years of letter writing. While LOGs are enriching, satisfying, and memorable, they take a bit of effort. Not just the candlepower necessary to compose something meaningful and heartfelt, but also soliciting the address, digging up the stamp, stationery, trudging to the post office, and so on. That's part of why they're so special. The recipient can see the letter writer has made a real effort to communicate and share feelings.

However, there is certainly a time and place to communicate in a much simpler fashion. Texting with a smartphone is a wonderful tool to keep in touch, say hello, make a quick inquiry, share an observation, and so on.

Word of warning: Not everyone is built for maintaining and fostering relationships. A large subsection of humanity is happy to let sleeping dogs lie, let marginal or former relationships slip away, leave the past in the past, and so on.

Look at it this way, for a snippet of anecdotal evidence: Most high school reunions only engage and attract a fraction of the graduating class. Maybe it's 25 percent, or maybe in closer-knit communities, it's closer to 40 percent. But the point is many or most invitees cannot be bothered, won't make the effort, live an inconvenient distance away, and just don't care. That's the hard truth of the matter and is a window into human nature. If this is your particular case, then the following advice will fall on deaf ears.

But a certain percentage of us attempt to heed the famous advice of Don Corleone in *The Godfather*. Said Vito Corleone, "Keep your friends close and your enemies closer." Personally speaking, I opt to think my enemies list could fit comfortably on a sticky note, or, worst case, an index card. But the preference is to keep in at least intermittent touch with scores upon scores of friends, associates, colleagues, and friendly acquaintances from the here and now and long ago. In that regard, texting is a wonderfully efficient tool.

It doesn't have to be (nor should it be) incessant. It doesn't have to be a regular thing. But there's a certain comfort in dropping a line every so often to those from your present, past, and way back. It could be once every few months; it could be once every year or two. Just a check-in, a simple "How ya doing?" This serves a dual purpose. The recipient will be tickled or touched that you were thinking of them. Concurrently, they are forced to think about you, at least in that moment, maybe just for a second, before resuming their hectic lives, or turning back to their crossword puzzle or daytime TV—whatever the case may be. But in either case, it's nice to be on somebody's mind, even for a moment.

A quick example: Maybe ten days ago, as these thoughts are being written, I was in my favorite New York–style deli in Salt Lake City, not far from home. There have been one hundred–something lunches there in the last decade, and consequently I've developed a friendly relationship with the owner. He wasn't on the premises that afternoon. But as the appetizing, overstuffed sandwich was delivered to my table, impulsively I snapped a photo and texted it to him, saying something like "Been absent for a bit, but the food is as good as ever!"

No response was forthcoming nor was one expected. But a chuckle ensued regardless, knowing it had taken just ten seconds to reach out to someone I like and admire to let him know he'd crossed my mind and was patronizing his business. It's a mini lesson referring to pillar one in the seven pillars of expressive gratitude—I sent the text to Mike because it made me feel good. Anything beyond that, the smile or nod he might've offered in reaction, is secondary—just collateral joy.

The other side of the coin—and it's happened to all of us: You run into a friend or acquaintance randomly. You quickly remark, "I've been thinking about you! I was just going to call (or text) you!" (Maybe you even meant it!) This happened to me maybe six weeks ago when I ran into a friendly acquaintance who's battling serious health issues. My intention to text him the day or two prior was legitimate, but it slipped through my mental grasp, and then we ran into each other. I felt like a fool and a fraud with my utterance, which was truly sincere. It's an unpleasant feeling, one that can be alleviated by the advice of a thousand Nike commercials we've all been subjected to: Just do it.

Try it sometime. Text away with a few different random people in your life. You might feel awkward for a beat in the doing. You might feel glum if there's no response forthcoming. But it's quick, easy-to-do, will give you a micro-flash of happiness in having reached out, and who knows? Perhaps you'll resurrect or reaffirm a long-moribund friendship or relationship by making that initial attempt.

For the scant amount of time it takes to make the minimal effort, it's certainly worth a try!

20

In Conclusion—
Twenty-Five Shallow Dives

About eight or ten letters into this hobby, back in early 2014, I commissioned custom stationery that I still use today. When a recipient opened the business-sized envelope they received in the mail, the *first thing* they would see (printed on the back of the stationery) was this quote from William Arthur Ward:

**Feeling gratitude and not expressing
it is like wrapping a present and not giving it.**

The fact is that hundreds of accomplished writers, statesmen, philosophers, theologians, and luminaries have given consideration to the concept of gratitude through the centuries. Here are two dozen worthwhile quotations on this subject, from some of the sharpest wits, deepest thinkers, finest minds, and successful individuals of the present and past:

Enjoy the little things, for one day you may look
back and realize they were the big things.

Robert Brautt

The only people with whom you should try to get even
are those who have helped you.

John E. Southard

You cannot do a kindness too soon because you
never know how soon it will be too late.

Ralph Waldo Emerson

We should certainly count our blessings, but we
should also make our blessings count.

Neal A. Maxwell

Silent gratitude isn't much use to anyone.

Gertrude Stein

If the only prayer you said in your whole life
was "thank you," that would suffice.

Meister Eckhart

Gratitude is the single most important ingredient
to living a successful and fulfilled life.

Jack Canfield

Let us be grateful to people who make us happy, they are
the charming gardeners who make our souls blossom.

Marcel Proust

There is a calmness to a life lived in gratitude, a quiet joy.

Ralph Blum

We must find time to stop and thank the people
who make a difference in our lives.

John F. Kennedy

The single greatest thing you can do to change your life today
would be to start being grateful for what you have right now.
And the more grateful you are, the more you get.

Oprah Winfrey

The chief idea of my life . . . is the idea of taking things
with gratitude, and not taking them for granted.

Gilbert K. Chesterton

Gratitude should be felt and experienced sincerely,
expressed generously and received graciously.

Michael Josephson

Since I'm not sure of the address to which to send
my gratitude, I put it out there in everything I do.

Michael J. Fox

So much has been given to me I have no time to
ponder over that which has been denied.

Helen Keller

What a wonderful life I've had!
I only wish I'd realized it sooner.

Sidonie Gabrielle Colette

When a person doesn't have gratitude, something
is missing from his or her humanity.

Elie Wiesel

We often take for granted the very things
that most deserve our gratitude.

Cynthia Ozick

Gratitude is the most exquisite form of courtesy.

Jacques Maritain

Showing gratitude is one of the simplest yet most
powerful things humans can do for each other.

Randy Pausch

Make it a habit to tell people thank you. To express your
appreciation, sincerely and without the expectation of
anything in return. Truly appreciate those around you,
and you'll soon find many others around you. Truly
appreciate life, and you'll find that you have more of it.

Ralph Marston

If ingratitude be numbered among the serious sins, then gratitude takes its place among the noblest of virtues.

Thomas S. Monson

One regret, dear world, that I am determined not to
have when I am lying on my deathbed is
that I did not kiss you enough.

Hafiz

Some people are always grumbling because roses have thorns;
I am thankful that thorns have roses.

Alphonse Karr

Appendix

The Letters in Total—Nearly Three Hundred and Counting

If you find it hard to wrap your head around the sum total of these letters, here they are, chronologically and alphabetically. If you're more of a visual person, imagine going to an office supply store, picking up a ream of copy paper, and dividing that thick stack in half. The bigger part of the stack is equal to the number of letters written and sent from November 2013 through October 2024.

When I first put this appendix together, the ebb and flow of the collection was striking. To wit: The total number of letters written in 2020 (the year my previous book, *Grateful*, was published) is equal to the total number of letters written in 2021 and 2022 *combined*.

It might have been ennui, a hangover from the previous book, or the stark realization of a long-held fear: Eventually there would be no more individuals to whom I felt deep gratitude.

But lo and behold, the momentum increased in 2023, and then the gratitude engine revved to unprecedented heights in 2024. Little more than three-quarters of the way through the year, I wrote more letters than in any previous year in totality, and significantly more than in 2021 and 2022 in combination. So much for the well running dry.

Some of this increased output is life circumstance. In 2024, there have been some "encore" letters, several gratitude/condolence letters, a pair of wedding wishes, some fare-thee-well letters, and so on.

A significant part of this output is attributable to the emotional, knee-jerk response to my Peruvian trauma. When the world turns sideways, some people drink, others do drugs, some might isolate or withdraw, and apparently, I reach out in my favorite fashion!

There are a handful of letters written and sent to public figures or luminaries through the years, although these are still mostly niche names to the wider world. Not so much A-list but more like B- or C-list. Suffice it to say names like Obama, Kardashian, Musk, or Messi are nowhere to be found!

In any event, this roster is included in its entirety to showcase how this delightful pastime can evolve into an all-consuming endeavor. If I can write nearly three hundred letters, anyone could and should write three, thirteen, or even thirty. But just start with that first one. You won't regret it.

Letters found in the chapter "One Dozen Sample Letters" are in italics.

2013

Ivan and Irena Boasher—Savannah friends

Paul de Vere—Former publisher

John Foley—High school buddy

Judith Z. Friedman—Sister

Evan and Tracy Harris—Brother-in-law and sister-in-law

Pat and Les Harris—In-laws

George Jorgenson—Savannah friend

Chaye Zuckerman Shapot—Sister

Dan Shepherd—Golf industry colleague

Brad Zola—NYC friend

Al Zuckerman—Brother

2014

Ed and Kim Damore—California friends

Amy Destephano—Sister-in-law

Kate Doran—Yoga friend

Hazel Durand—Old friend

Tony and Donna Eicholz—Savannah acquaintances

Sara Fein—Childhood friend

Michael Gibson—Business associate

Kevin Hammer—Golf associate

Laurie Hammer—PGA professional

Herb Kandel—Uncle

Kayla Z. Kantor—Daughter

Scott Lauretti—Business associate

Debby and Barry Luskey—Savannah friends

Angela McSwain and Steve Wilmot—Golf industry colleagues

Karli Z. Meredith—Daughter

Elizabeth Miller—Savannah acquaintance

Mike Morgan—PGA professional
Fred Muller—PGA professional
Kyle Poplin—Former editor
Larry Pritika—College buddy
Dave Ryan—High school buddy
Emily Summers—Ski industry acquaintance
Sweet Potatoes Waitresses—Favorite waitstaff
Mike Whitaker—Golf buddy
Rick and Sue Wohler—Savannah friends
Elaine H. Zuckerman—Wife

2015

Kendall Beene—Yoga teacher
Jim Crawford—Savannah friend
Ashley Dodd—Yoga teacher
Ryan Duffy and Bryan Icenhower—Business associates
Laura Feller—Family friend
Dave Gaudreau—College buddy
Paul Grassey—Savannah acquaintance
Mike Greenberg and Mike Golic—TV personalities
Craig Hafer—Park City friend
John and Mindy Halsey—Park City friends
Mike Harmon—PGA professional
Earl Haynes—Savannah friend
Rich Katz—Golf industry colleague
Cynthia Key and Karen Lynch—Park City friends
Brad King—Golf industry colleague
Bill and Tina Kropp—Savannah friends
Bernice Luskey—Mother of a friend
Caitlin Martz—Ski industry acquaintance

Eric Nadelman—Hometown friend
Jess Neeley—Savannah friend
Steve Snyders—Golf industry colleague
Dave Stockton—PGA professional
Sloan Thompson—Savannah friend
Gail Thurston and Charles Morgan—Savannah friends

2016

Paul Berman—Home builder
Susan and Mark Berti—NYC friends
Ken Carter—NYC friend
JR Chase—Childhood friend
Michele Cone—Park City friend
Janeen Driscoll—Golf industry colleague
Pete and Alice Dye—Golf industry colleagues
Julia Friedman—Niece
Tom Harack—Golf industry colleague
Jean-Yves Lacroix—Home architect
Dave Levine—Park City friend
Rose and Fred Malunes—Savannah restaurateurs
Jim Melody—College buddy
Jay Michelman—Hometown friend
Stephanie Mobley and Kim Norvell—Yoga teachers
Brian Oar—Utah friend
Susan Pearlstine—South Carolina friend
Alyssa Perkins—Park City friend
Dave Rafus—Casual acquaintance
Joe Rice—Golf industry colleague
Tim Riviere—College buddy
Fred Rubinfeld—Park City friend

Bill Safrin—PGA professional
Joe Shaffel—Savannah acquaintance
Michael Shapot—Brother-in-law
Kip Van Valkenburg—Park City friend
Kara Webster—Home designer
Katie Wright—Park City friend

2017

Ken Boardman—College buddy
Karen Christenson—Business associate
Martin Coleman—Former advisor
Katie Foley-Kangalu and Seware Kangalu—Newlyweds
Cheryl Henry—Widow
Kevin Johnson—Casual acquaintance
Jonathan Kantor—Son-in-law
Jared Kelowitz—Golf industry colleague
Noah Luskey—Savannah friend
Trish McLeod—Savannah friend
John McNeely—PGA professional
Kevin Meredith—Son-in-law
Rich Nadelman—Hometown friend
Teri Orr and Moe Hickey—Park City acquaintances
Park City Toastmasters Club
Jim and Georgine Scott—Savannah friends
Kelly Shea—Widow
Steve Smith—High school acquaintance
Elizabeth Spratley and Steven Provere—Wedding planners
Ed Stambovsky—Hometown friend
Joe and Janet Steffen—Savannah acquaintances
"Team K"—Daughter and son-in-law
Kate Zuckerman—Niece

2018

Bill Check—Savannah acquaintance

Amy Lu Christopherson—Massage therapist

John Concannon—Park City friend

Michele and Dan Cone—Park City friends

Peter Crosby—High school buddy

Jana Dalton—Park City friend

Joann Dost—Golf industry colleague

David Ellsworth—College buddy

John Farrell—PGA professional

Leonard Finkel—Golf industry colleague

David Gaskin—Savannah physician

Doug Goldstein—Savannah friend

Kelly Gordon—Savannah friend

Pam Grayboff—Childhood friend

Jerry Gross—Park City friend

Charlie Hope—Savannah friend

Matt Kaiser—Park City friend

Kayla Z. Kantor II—Daughter

Dr. Lillian Khor—Salt Lake City cardiologist

Chris Klein—Savannah attorney

Longmeadow High School 40th Reunion Committee

Larry and Laurie Pritika—College friends

Stacy Schlafstein—Savannah friend

Steve Washuta—Savannah acquaintance

2019

Laurie Banks—Park City friend

Devrin and Jane Carlson-Smith—Park City friends

Kristen Case—Park City friend

Brent Clapacs—Park City friend

Mark Cohen—High school buddy

Greg and Karen Conway—Park City friends

Deer Crest Club Crew—Cadre of young workers

Lori Draymore—Childhood friend

Valerie Edgemon—Widow

Cami Foley—College buddy

Judith Z. Friedman II—Sister

George Geisser—Savannah friend

Tom Hale—Casual acquaintance

Tommy Halsey—Son of a friend

Tracy Harris—Sister-in-law

Bill Huffman—Golf industry colleague

Eric and Amy Kamisher—Park City friends

Jodi Kantor—In-law

Sue Ann Kern and Gregg Davidson—Park City friends

Knight and Knight Dental—Dental practice

Tim and Lisa O'Brien—Park City friends

Nate Overholser—Savannah friend

Ashley Pennewell—Park City friend

Bruce and Kathy Petersen—Park City friends

Jody and Kenneth Sadler—Savannah acquaintances

Chaye Shapot and Judith Friedman parting letter—Sisters

Krista Traxler—Casual acquaintance

Diego Zegarra—Park City friend

2020

Marty Bauer and George Parker—Club officials

Russ Cable—Business associate

Ted Cho—Advisor

Perry Dye—Golf industry colleague

Hal Ginsburg—NYC friend
Leah Harris—Niece
Kayla Kantor III—Daughter
Kayla and Jonathan Kantor—Daughter and son-in-law
Maureen Mekjian—Park City friend
Leslie Meredith—Granddaughter
Troy Michaud—Park City friend
Mister Sister Trio—Local musical group
Bruce Morra—Park City friend
Michelle Rayner—Book designer
Dallen Root and Ryan Forsyth—Park City acquaintances
Eric and Jane Sagerman—Park City friends
Israel Schepps—Hometown buddy
Isaac Shapot—Nephew
Andrew Smith—Myofascial release therapist
Janice Stambovsky—Widow
Jessie Valdez—Salt Lake City acquaintance
Tyler Young—High School buddy

2021
Katherine Cardali—Mother of a friend
Tonya Cumbee—Park City friend
Erin Grady—Ski industry colleague
Pete Holschuh—College buddy
Steve and Deb Marcus—Massachusetts friends
Karen Massimino—NYC friend
Kirsten McDonough—Widow
Nic Pigati—Casual acquaintance
Debbie Smith—High school acquaintance
Charlie Sturgis—Park City friend

Cari Welliver—Park City friend
Larry and Sheree Zaslavsky—Savannah friends

2022
Patrice Clapacs—Park City friend
Stephen Gallup—Club manager
Hannah Kearney—Park City acquaintance
Lindsey Mattison—Pilates instructor
Rory McIlroy—PGA Tour professional
Rob and Laura Medway—Park City friends
Cathy Morra—Widow
Jane and Eric Sagerman II—Park City friends
Rick and Linda Smaligo—Park City friends

2023
Dirk Bak—Park City friend
Molly Blewett—Park City friend
Wendell Brown—Park City friend
John Burke—Park City friend
Good Movement Studio—Pilates instructors
John Halsey—Park City friend
Evan and Tracy Harris II—Brother-in-law and sister-in-law
Offir Horn—Israeli tour guide
Karen Hylwa—Business associate
Brad Kaufman—Park City friend
Rick and Deb Latham—New Hampshire acquaintances
Karli Meredith and Jonathan Kantor—Daughter
and son-in-law
Rob Parry—Park City friend
Kathy and Bruce Petersen II—Park City friends

Malen Pierson—Artist friend
Shane Sharp—Golf industry colleague
Michael Zaccaro—Business associate

2024

Randy Baron and Autumn Bear—Park City friends
Ted Bezemer—Physical therapist and trainer
Dawnette Cabaluna—Spa director
Devrin and Jane Carlson-Smith II—Park City friends
Maury Davis—Widow
Amy Destephano II—Sister-in-law
Amy Destephano III—Sister-in-law
Ben Edgar—Concierge extraordinaire
Emily and Gavin Fine—Texas friends
EJ and Mary Kay Foody—Florida acquaintances
John Fry—Park City friend
Christa Graff—Park City friend
Bob and Jen Gurss—Park City friends
Charlie Halsey—Son of a friend
Michael Harkins—Park City friend
Mike Harmon II—PGA professional
Pat Harris—Mother-in-Law
Pat and Les Harris II—In-laws
Rachel Israel—Widow
Ron Jackenthal—Park City friend
Brandon Judd—Physical therapist
Ethan Kantor—Grandson
Sue Ann Kern—Park City friend
Noah Luskey and Bootsie Heffernan—Newlyweds
Heather and Rob Mansson—Park City acquaintances

Dan McBride—Park City friend
Chad Mobeley—Videographer
Gregg Novick—College buddy
Lisa and Tim O'Brien II—Park City friends
Andy Peiffer—Salt Lake City physician
Ashley Pennewell and Joey Krueger—Newlyweds
Jarrod Ross—Park City acquaintance
Brian Schott—Montana friend
Jennifer Sharp—Widow
Rick and Linda Smaligo II—Park City friends
Kaitlyn Taylor—Park City friend
Elaine Zuckerman II—Wife

About the Author

Author Photography by Brad Lewis

Joel Zuckerman has written ten books and nearly three hundred Letters of Gratitude. He is the only two-time recipient of the Book of the Year Award bestowed by the International Network of Golf. For twenty-plus years, he wrote about golf, travel, and a wide range of sports and activities for more than one hundred different publications and websites. These include *Sports Illustrated*, Delta's *Sky Magazine*, *Continental*, *Maxim*, and *Millionaire*.

As a speaker, he has been engaged by luxury cruise lines, and at corporate retreats, conferences, and country clubs on three continents. Joel, his wife, Elaine, and their family reside amid the mountains of northern Utah.